What Astrology is
...and How to Use it

What Astrology is
...and How to Use it

Bruce Scofield

THE WESSEX ASTROLOGER

Published in 2021 by
The Wessex Astrologer Ltd
PO Box 9307
Swanage
BH19 9BF

For a full list of our titles go to www.wessexastrologer.com

© Bruce Scofield 2021
Bruce Scofield asserts his moral right to be recognised as
the author of this work

ISBN 9781910531624
Originally published as *User's Guide to Astrology* by
One Reed Publications in 1987, 1997 and 2020
under ISBN 0962803138

Charts created using Solar Fire by Astrolabe Inc.

Cover design by Andy Jay

A catalogue record for this book is available at The British Library

No part of this book may be reproduced or used in any form or by any means without the written permission of the publisher.
A reviewer may quote brief passages.

Table of Contents

Foreword	ix
Preface	xi
1. Astrology for Open Minds	**1**
Astrology: Science or Art?	1
Scientific Research on Astrology	4
Astrology and the Scientific Community	6
Common Objections to Astrology	8
A Mechanism for Astrology	13
Astrology and Religion	16
2. What Astrologers Do	**19**
Natural Astrology	19
Judicial Astrology	20
The Astrological Chart	21
Interpreting the Astrological Chart	22
Forecasting with Astrology	23
The Philosophy of an Astrologer	25
What Makes a Good Astrologer?	25
3. The History of Astrology	**27**
Ancient Mesopotamia	28
India, China and Mesoamerica	28
Ancient Greece	29
Ancient Rome	30
After the Fall of Rome	31
The Renaissance and the fate of astrology	32
The Reformation	33

What Astrology is ...And How to Use it

The Loss of Royal Patronage	34
The Split Between Astrology and Astronomy	35
The Rise of Modern Science	37
Other Factors in the Decline	39
Astrology Revived	40
4. The Planets and Other Points	**42**
The Astronomy of the Solar System	43
The Sun	45
The Moon	46
The Inner Planets	47
The Asteroids	51
Jupiter and Saturn	52
Chiron: A Transitional Object	54
The Outer Planets	54
Planets beyond Pluto	58
The Primary Planets and their Astrological Meanings	58
The Ephemeris	62
Other Points Used in Astrology	63
5. Aspects and Alignments	**66**
The Principal Aspects: Harmonics 1 through 12	68
Parallels and Contraparallels	72
Hard vs. Soft Aspects	72
Major vs. Minor Aspects	72
Applying, Separating, and Orbs	73
Aspects and Cycles	74
A Summary of the Aspects	74
Midpoints	76
6. Signs of the Zodiac	**77**
Why Twelve Signs?	77
The Zodiac and the Seasons	78
The Quadruplicities or Qualities	79

The Triplicities or Elements	80
The Polarities	80
The Signs through the Year	81
Descriptions of the Signs	83
Affinities with the Planets	96
Dignities and Debilities	97
7. Houses: Sectors of Sky	**99**
The Ascendant and MC Axes	101
House Systems	103
What the Houses Show	104
Meanings of the Houses	105
A Personal Zodiac	108
The Planets in the Houses	109
The astrological chart	111
Hemisphere Emphasis	113
Relocating the Houses: Astro-Mapping	115
8. Reading a Birth Chart	**116**
What Psychologists Look For	121
Building an Astrological Personality Profile	123
Ten Personality Traits	127
General Planetary Distribution	133
Astrology and Self-Knowledge	134
Fate and Free-Will	136
Relationships	137
9. Predicting with Transits	**142**
Learning About Transits: An Exercise	143
The Transits of the Planets	146
The Seven-Year Cycle	150
The Graphic Ephemeris	151
Symbolic Substitution	153
Other Astrological Predictive Techniques	154

10. Following the planets	**157**
Choosing the Best Time to Take Action	158
The Angularity of Jupiter, Sun and Venus	161
Mercury Retrograde	162
Using Mutual Aspects	165
The Aspects of the Major Planets: Mundane Astrology	166
Appendix A: The Astrological Reading	171
Appendix B: Astrology Software	175
Appendix C: Calculating an Astrological Chart	184
Appendix D: An Astrological Resource Directory	195

Foreword

At the present time, astrology holds a very low status in the dominant culture. Writers and editors of magazines generally ignore the subject and studiously avoid even using the word in any context other than negative or deprecating. Television executives rarely allow the subject to be televised, and then only as entertainment. Scientists and professors attack the subject at regular intervals, using the same old arguments. Intelligent responses from astrologers are almost always suppressed. Colleges won't allow the subject to be taught, and any professors who show the slightest interest in it are ostracized, if not demoted or denied promotion. Scientific studies that show proof for astrology's claims are pushed under the rug. Only on Wall Street, where greed is king, does astrology sometimes get a hearing, and then only because it is perceived as an asset in the rush to material riches. In short, astrology is a banished subject, an underground study. On the surface it appears to have little or no influence on the cultural mainstream.

Reasons why the dominant culture has rejected astrology can be found in two of the underlying assumptions of Western civilization. One of these is that certain doctrines of the monotheistic religions concerning human freedom, and these go back centuries, require rejection of any influence of the planets. These doctrines have a complex history, but suffice it to say that intermediaries between humans and God (except maybe for angels) are a problem theologically.

Astrology is also rejected by religion because it is interpreted to deny free-will. This is far from the truth. Astrology actually offers a deeper view into behavior, personality and character. It describes how humans, embedded in nature, are affected by the cosmic environment of the solar system. This is valuable information that informs, not limits, the choices we make. In astrology, cosmic influences are there to be studied and have no bearing on God or diminish free-will, certainly not more than genetics or childhood upbringing do.

The second reason lies in the assumptions of reductionist, mechanistic and materialist technology-driven science, which are that nature can only be understood in its parts, not its full manifestation. These are the same reasons why alternative medicine and traditional natural healing which treat the body holistically have been ignored. These reasons explain resistance to the deeper messages of environmentalism that promote sustainability, and likewise the 350-year effort to eliminate or marginalize Native American cultures and their ecological approach to nature.

Put simply, the fundamental assumptions that drive Western culture tend to suppress subjects that do not conform to a mechanistic model or see humans as a part nature. Western religions have regarded humanity as separate from nature, a special creation. Much of modern science, in the service of politicians and corporations, and propelled by the assumptions of modern capitalism, promotes an official agenda that ultimately supports a righteous dominance of man over nature. The unquestioned assumption in much technology-driven science, which is essentially the same as in Western religion, is that nature is there to be conquered, manipulated, and exploited. This is how it has been for centuries, though there are now some signs that this anti-nature program is being forced to change.

Astrology offers a view of life and the world that is inclusive, cosmic in scope, humbling, inspiring, and a challenge to some of our deepest assumptions about what is really going on in our lives. Astrology takes the dynamism of our cosmic environment and expresses it as a practical guide or road map for living and a power tool for expanding awareness. Use it intelligently.

Preface

Today, there are books about astrology covering every aspect of the subject, including its practice, history, and philosophical implications. This book attempts to cover a wide range of topics. For those who want to develop a general understanding of the subject without investing in a lot of books, this guidebook is a good start. Readers with a scientific background may find its practical information useful, as well as the section on the history of astrology and the arguments raised against it. There are also many people who have no intention of becoming astrologers, but merely want to "try it at home" and would like a handy general reference on astrology. Exercises in astrological prediction and a simple technique for analyzing a birth chart are included that can meet these needs. This material is pragmatic, and may appeal to those with experimental inclinations. As the title suggests, the purpose of *What Astrology is… and How to Use It* is to guide one through the full range of the subject. It does not pretend to be an exhaustive account, just a practical overview. The suggested reading in Appendix D will direct interested readers toward more complex and specialized works.

This guide began in 1981 as a twelve-page booklet entitled *Some Facts about Astrology*. In 1984, I expanded it to forty pages, adding hand-out material I had been using in classes and lectures. Then I retitled it *Astrology for Open Minds* and printed several hundred copies. In 1987, I expanded the text to one hundred pages, keeping the same basic format, and changed the name to *User's Guide to Astrology*. In 1997 I revised the book once again, this time with an ISBN number and had 3,000 copies printed. The book sold well at first and continued to sell slowly for many years afterward. In 2018

I began the process of re-formatting the text which had been stored on a floppy disk for the previous 20 years. Editing of the text in 2020 led to this latest incarnation, the fifth edition, of what seems to be a book with a life of its own, a factual, non-ideological guidebook of astrology that began 40 years ago.

1
Astrology for Open Minds

Dictionaries define astrology as a study that attempts to understand the affairs of human beings by studying the stars and planets. In essence, astrology is exactly that – but it is also more. First and foremost, it is a subject that, in addition to practice, includes theory, research, and its own history. Most people associate the subject with its practice, however, and for good reason. What practicing astrologers do is interpret a map of the sky computed for the time and place of birth to discover information about a person's character and likely destiny. This is really quite remarkable and unmatched by any other subject. The map they use is commonly called a horoscope, though astrological chart is a more accurate name. The positions of the planets in the birth chart function as symbols of a person's basic character, prominent personality traits, and can also be used to time major life events. A good astrologer is even able to deduce something about a person's spouse, parents, children, and even pets from their astrological chart. According to the prevailing belief systems of modern Western society, this should be impossible. A vast gulf separates those who embrace and practice astrology and those who do not. Before we get into the nuts and bolts of astrology itself, let's examine the controversial issues that surround the subject and try to answer the central question; "is astrology real or fake?"

Astrology: Science or Art?

In the minds of skeptics, astrology is a pseudo-science, a subject that pretends to be a science. If this label means that there is no scientific foundation whatsoever for astrology, then the skeptics are either un-informed or have fallen for a cover-up that will be explained further on. If pseudo-science means that astrology does not entirely follow strict scientific methodologies, then the same accusation could be made against diagnostic medicine or psychotherapy. Both of these fields use a combination of scientific method (or technology) and personal judgment calls. We all know that some doctors and therapists are simply much better than others. If the individual human element was taken out of medicine and all doctors and psychologists followed a strict set of scientific rules, we'd all be the worse for it. If the skeptic's standards for scientific worthiness were applied to the practice of medicine and psychology, these subjects would probably join astrology in the rejection bin. This suggests that the skeptics don't know what they are talking about, so we must ask what exactly is astrology and how does it differ from accepted studies like medicine and psychology that have what are considered legitimate connections to science?

To understand astrology, it is important to keep in mind that it is very different from the "hard" sciences like physics or chemistry. These sciences seek precise relationships between measurements and mathematics. Astrology uses mathematics to precisely measure the positions of the planets and their relationships to each other, but practitioners must contend with a constantly changing solar system configuration. No two birth charts can ever be the same. This requires astrology to be more like psychology and medicine, where scientific methodologies are applied to the human condition but estimates and deductions must be made. Like psychology and medicine, the practice of astrology should be understood as a diagnostic art that uses scientific data.

The only thing strictly scientific about astrology then is the astronomy that is needed to create the schematic map of the sky – the astrological chart. Astrologers use astronomical data, mathematics, and computers to determine precisely how the sky was or will be configured at a given place and time. The rest of the work is basically intelligent interpretation of data which usually improves with experience. A close parallel to this kind of process would be a doctor's diagnosis of illness – after a careful reading of several scientific tests (eg. CT scan, MRI) and laboratory data (blood test), personal experience and estimates often shape judgment.

An understanding of astrology as interpretation of scientific data begins with the concept that it is basically a system, code, or language that uses a set of symbols: the Sun, Moon and planets, zodiac signs, houses, and aspects. Over the course of astrology's long history these symbols have been found to correspond with very specific categories of things, events, and personality traits. An astrologer blends combinations of these symbols and makes deductions about a person or situation. This act of interpretation is more art than science. Astrology also differs from much of modern science because it uses a different kind of thinking, one that assumes that things are interconnected. Mainstream science, which breaks its subject matter into pieces and extracts them from their environment, focuses on separations and boundaries that can be measured exactly. Astrology is holistic and works with repeating patterns, connections and linkages and is concerned with inter-connectedness – the ecology of body, mind and spirit on this planet. There is a branch of science that strives to understand nature in this way, however. It is the science of systems, which includes topics like cybernetics, chaos, and complexity, all of which take into account interconnections, linkages and patterns.[1] A certain class of phenomena, what are called self-organizing systems (body, mind, personality, group behaviors, etc.), which are the phenomena that astrology works with, is better understood when approached from a systems perspective. Mainstream science, which approaches problems by reducing them into parts, has been less successful in explaining and working with self-organizing systems.

Astrology is sometimes attacked because much of it seems archaic to those trained in the modern sciences that originated only in the last few centuries. The signs of the zodiac still retain their ancient names,

---

1   See works by Fritjof Capra and Ervin Laszlo.

and concepts like planetary rulership and house position are still a major part of the subject. Astrology has retained connections to an earlier time when humans were not so separate from nature. These ideas of the interconnectedness of life and its surrounding cosmic environment are similar to some ideas held today in the life sciences, ecology and the environmentalist movement. Modern astrology, while it has built on more than 4,000 years of observations, has also been continually challenged and updated. Just as ancient medicine is not the medicine practiced today, ancient Greek, Roman, Medieval or Renaissance astrology is not the astrology of the 21st century.

Scientific Research on Astrology

Astrology hypothesizes that there is some form of correlation between the positions of celestial objects and the biological and meteorological processes on Earth. In support of this hypothesis, there exists today a modest body of scientific research, most of it statistical. Partly because of a prejudice against astrology, the history of which is described in Chapters 3 and 4, funding for astrological research has not been forth-coming, and progress in finding supportive scientific evidence has been slow. For the time being, astrologers and supporters of astrology can cite only a few studies that clearly demonstrate that at least some parts of astrology are real and measurable. The most famous of these studies are those done by the French statisticians Michel Gauquelin and Francoise Schneider-Gauquelin.

Beginning in the mid-1950s and continuing through to the 1980s, the Gauquelins published a number of books and reports on their statistical studies of astrology. Their research centered on the effects of planets on profession, personality traits, and heredity. Since ancient times, astrologers have claimed that the location of a planet, in its daily rising and setting, at the time of a person's birth indicates its potential to affect that individual's personality and life. The Gauquelins began their study by first accumulating birth data on thousands of people and then determining where each planet was located relative to the horizon at the time and place of birth. For example, for a person born at noon, the Sun would be in the middle of the sky overhead; at dusk, on the western horizon. The same kind of analysis was done for the Moon, Mercury, Venus, Mars, Jupiter, and Saturn.

In one study, done in 1955, Michel Gauquelin plotted the position of Mars relative to the horizon for a sample of 2,000 sports champions. (According to astrology, Mars is associated symbolically with war, competition and sports.) If there were no planetary effect, one would expect Mars to be randomly distributed in the sample. Instead, the study showed that Mars was situated more often in the sectors located just after rising, setting, upper culmination, and lower culmination. A control group of people who were not sports champions showed an even distribution of Mars through the sky. The Gauquelins found similar correlations for Saturn in the birth charts of scientists, Jupiter with famous actors, Venus with writers, and the Moon with writers and politicians.

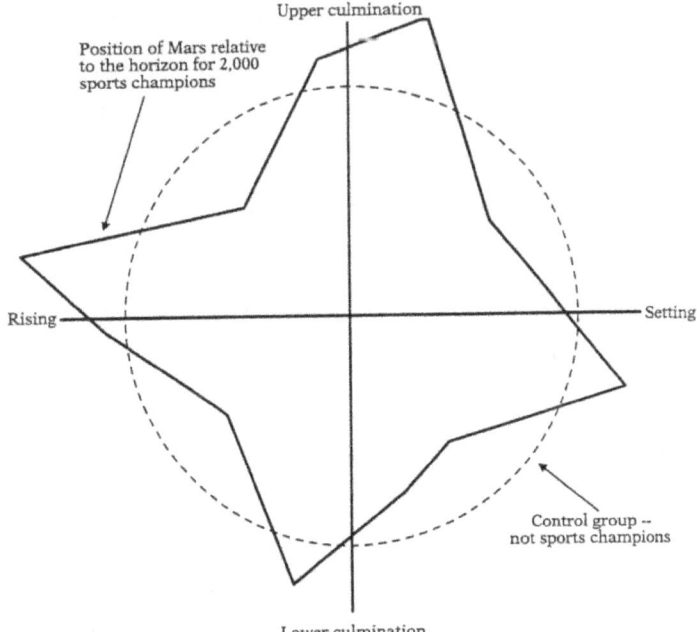

Figure 1. Gauquelin Research

The Gauquelins conducted many similar studies looking for correlations between known facts about a group of people and the location of a particular planet at the time of birth.[2] They also found what appears to be evidence of a kind of planetary heredity: a planet located in one of the emphasized sectors of the sky tended to be duplicated in the birth charts of offspring. In later studies by the Gauquelins, personality traits showed an even clearer correlation than profession did. These studies suggested that the real link with the planets is with personality, not profession, which is usually a choice dictated by personality.

The Gauquelin work shows that certain astrological principles can be demonstrated through rather complex and time-consuming statistical studies. Other tenets of astrology are more difficult to test because of the individual nature of each astrological chart and the different interpretation styles used by experienced astrologers. Statistical testing in the field of psychology is similarly difficult and controversial due to the complex nature of human personality. The big difference between psychological and astrological scientific studies is that the former gets plenty of funding and institutional support, the later is done by independent researchers who bear the costs themselves. Because research can be extremely complex, time-consuming, and costly, most topics in astrology remain to be tested.

Astrology and the Scientific Community

The Gauquelin findings were successfully replicated many times, both by themselves and by independent statisticians. Nevertheless, their work has so far made little impact on the scientific community. To give you some idea of the limitations imposed on astrology and astrologers by skeptics, here is the story of their reaction to the Gauquelin studies.

In 1975, *The Humanist* magazine dedicated the 100th anniversary of the American Ethical Union to the discrediting of astrology. On the very first

---

2   See any of Gauquelin's many books that describe the research.

pages of the September/October issue was a list of 186 scientists, including 18 Nobel prize winners, who had signed a statement saying that astrology was essentially superstition and that there was no verifiable scientific basis for a belief in it. The rest of the issue included a number of anti-astrology articles.

One of the articles in *The Humanist* attacked the methodology of the Gauquelin's astrological experiments. Michel Gauquelin responded by challenging the skeptics to replicate the experiments. The Committee for the Scientific Investigation of the Claims of the Paranormal (CSICOP), a kind of self-appointed scientific thought-police, agreed to do this. They soon made public their conclusions – that Gauquelin's claims were false. This announcement was loudly broadcasted in the media. For several years, numerous articles and stories appeared in magazines and newspapers reporting that the scientists were absolutely correct about Gauquelin's statistical studies being faulty. But also during this period, one of the original CSICOP skeptics resigned and published evidence that the CSICOP replications of Gauquelin's experiments actually agreed with his conclusions, and that this fact had been covered up.[3] Gauquelin, realizing that he was dealing with a situation that was far from scientific, pressed on and was eventually vindicated after several independently conducted studies checked and confirmed the correctness of his work. Soon after, some scientists submitted a tiny notice to *The Skeptical Inquirer* (Spring 1983), reporting that Gauquelin's studies had withstood their challenge. But most of the general public, which had heard all the negative attacks on astrology, never heard the eventual outcome of this debate.

Historians of science have long observed that so-called "scientific truths" can change over time. What was believed to be true 100 years ago may now be considered false. What was false 100 years ago may now be considered truth. Science, like all human endeavors, is strongly affected by dominant personalities who have personal reasons for keeping things a certain way. While scientific methods may point to the need for a change in thinking,

---

3   *Fate* magazine, October 1981.

historians know that a scientific revolution is more likely to occur when the supporters of the older view die or retire. Good examples of this can be found in the resistance that established scientists have had, and still have, to supposedly radical concepts like holistic and alternative medicine, the self-sustaining properties of the biosphere (Gaia hypothesis), and intelligence in the higher primates (gorillas, chimpanzees, and orangutans). Strong evidence is never enough for obstructers of progress who use the banner of science to preserve their respectability and often dominant personalities will have it their way. We are dealing with something like this in regard to the Gauquelin tests of astrology.

Today, the main attackers of astrology are self-appointed militant skeptics and ambitious clergy, and in nearly every case these people know next to nothing about the subject. Maintaining that their definition of reality is demonstrably the only one, they use their positions of authority to silence their critics. For centuries they have used the same arguments against astrology. Though they have tarnished its reputation and kept it out of the intellectual mainstream, and consequently out of funding, for the past three hundred years, they have not been able to completely eliminate it. Let's now take a look at these perennial arguments.

Common Objections to Astrology

The most common objections raised by the critics of astrology are: the problem of the two zodiacs, the question of the destinies of twins, fate vs. free-will, and the lack of a scientific explanation for how astrology works. Let's look at these issues more closely.

The Two Zodiacs

The most recognizable part of astrology today is the zodiac, the 12-fold division of the path that the Sun and planets follow in their movements through the sky. The zodiacal sign in which the Sun was positioned at a person's birth has come to be known as his or her "sign." For many people, this is all the astrology they are ever exposed to. Newspapers and magazines, in their efforts to interest as many people as possible, devote regular columns to this sort of astrological interpretation. In the history of astrology, these Sun-sign "horoscopes," which promote a simplistic view of the subject, are a relatively recent phenomena.

Most Western astrologers use the tropical zodiac which is tied to the cycle of the seasons and measures the ratio of day to night over the course of a year. The beginning of this zodiac of *signs* is the point where the Sun is found on the first day of spring in the Northern Hemisphere, a date when the lengths of day and night are equal. Astronomers use a sidereal zodiac, as do astrologers in India and some Western astrologers. This is the zodiac of *constellations* and it is tied to the relatively unchanging positions of these groupings of stars. About 2,000 years ago, these two types of zodiacs coincided – the signs of the zodiac were the constellations. Since that time, a slow movement of Earth's axis has caused the two types of zodiacs to separate by about 26 degrees. This westward movement of the vernal point (where the Sun is on the first day of spring) through the constellations is known as the *precession of the equinoxes*. It is this movement which gives rise to the notion of the astrological "ages." According to many astrologers, we are presently near the end of the age of Pisces and approaching the age of Aquarius, due to begin in a century or so. This topic, however, is still under discussion by astrologers and there are many conflicting opinions as to exactly when this change of ages will occur and how it might correlate with history.

The tropical zodiac of signs divides the year into twelfths, with key points at the beginning of the seasons. Each twelfth occupies 30 degrees of the Sun's path through the sky as seen from Earth. These 12 spatial divisions are the familiar zodiac signs which are said to modify, like a filter, the influence of the Sun, Moon, and any planet located within them. The tropical zodiac has nothing to do with the constellations made up of stars, though it does relate to the seasons and the fact that we have 12 months in our year.

The sidereal zodiac used by astronomers is a division of the year based on the location of the Sun in groups of stars called constellations. Since the constellations are not all of equal size, the time that the Sun spends in one of them varies. Technically, there are actually 13 constellations that intercept the Sun's path; the 12 constellations of the ancient zodiac plus the constellation Ophiuchus, a small part of which is located between Scorpio and Sagittarius. Periodically, astronomers intent on debunking astrology will announce to the media that astrologers haven't noticed that there is a 13th sign. Because the media and the public are so poorly informed about astrology, they haven't noticed that these astronomers are really quite ignorant of the fact that it is the tropical zodiac that astrologers use. Further, the zodiac is not necessarily a required component of astrology except in the sense of locating the positions of the planets. A zodiac is a spatial framework used to measure the position of an astronomical body. If a birth chart could be compared to a meal set on a table, a change of zodiacs would be comparable to a change of tablecloths. Both the dinner spread and the table itself would remain in the same place relative to each other, though the backdrop would be different.

The influence of the tropical zodiac of signs, which has traditionally been said to modify the basic nature of the Sun, Moon, and planets, has not yet been conclusively proven scientifically.[4] Separating the influences of the Sun, Moon, and planets in order to measure them presents serious problems for the researcher. However, several studies done by astrologer Jeff Mayo and psychologist Hans J. Eysenck found that different zodiacal positions of the Sun appears to correlate with introversion and extroversion in personality. Their work, which has been disputed, seems to confirm the traditional astrological notion that the fire and Air signs tend to be extroverted while the Water and Earth signs are introverted. While these studies are certainly important, many principles of astrology stand independent of any zodiac. It is unfortunate that the public has come to associate the entire field of

---

4   Differences in personality have been found to be correlated to differences in season of birth according to the subdiscipline called "seasonal biology."

astrology with the tropical zodiac, and to believe that the subject should either stand or fall according to the validity of zodiacal Sun-signs. In fact, certain schools of astrology, notably Cosmobiology and the Hamburg School founded by Alfred Witte, are able to give complete readings of astrological charts without any reference at all to the influence of zodiacal signs.

Twins, Fate, and Free-Will

Another common argument brought against astrology concerns twins. Critics ask, how can twins be different if they were born at the same place and at nearly the same time? Interestingly, the astrologer's answer to this question gives insight into the fate versus free-will problem, a stumbling block for many trying to evaluate astrology and a common point of attack by the clergy for centuries.

There is much evidence that identical twins separated at birth very often follow a strikingly similar path. There are many dramatic reports, past and present, of separated twins leading almost exactly parallel lives. The University of Minnesota has long researched twins and has noted this strange phenomenon. Of course, scientists attribute these similarities to genetics; ignoring astrological configurations in the birth chart. While twins raised apart show similarities, twins who are raised together are often quite dissimilar in personality and life progress. These differences may be evidence of free-will. Astrologers suggest that separated identical twins follow similar life patterns, ones that were imprinted at birth and symbolized in the birth chart, and that they do this quite naturally because their individual identities are not threatened by being in constant contact and competition with each other. Astrologers note that twins not separated will typically choose different parts of their birth charts around which to build an identity. For example, consider identical twins born when the Sun was in Gemini and the Moon was in Taurus. One twin might focus primarily on Gemini and build her identity around that sign's characteristics and become a teacher. The other twin would then construct her identity around the motivations and themes symbolized by Taurus and might become a banker.

Twins raised together often exhibit synchronicity in their life patterns on a very basic level. For example, an astrologer might forecast that both twins would have a relationship crisis at a certain time. At the designated time, one twin marries and the other separates from a relationship. Is this a case of astrological failure? The astrologer would argue it wasn't by pointing out that both twins had to confront relationship issues at the designated time. The fact that each chose a different path is further proof of free-will. While astrology suggests that we follow a precise timetable symbolized by the distribution and positions of the planets at the time and place of our birth, it also shows that we can make our own decisions and exert our own will if we choose. For astrologers, twins illustrate the fact that we have freedom of choice – if we want it.

One of the assumptions usually made in regard to twin births is that they both have the same astrological chart. From a broad astrological perspective, that is true, and that accounts for the similarities between twins. However, technical experts in astrology would argue that a separation of even one minute of time between the births can account for some significant differences. For example, one twin could be born with the last degree of Aries rising, and the other, born only one minute later, could have the first degree of Taurus rising. While the arc separating the births is small, the sign difference is great, and this would signify very different identities. Astrologers would also point out that a difference of four minutes between births can account for a year's difference in the timing of a major life event. One twin might experience a certain kind of stress at a developmentally vulnerable time. The other could experience the stress a year later and consequently have a very different experience. There are other techniques in astrology, including midpoint analysis and harmonic charts, that reveal significant differences between astrological charts separated by very small amounts of time.

A Mechanism for Astrology

The question scientists most often ask in regard to astrology is "how does it work"? The short answer is that no one really knows how it works, but astrologers have learned how to work with it. This is not so different from the commonplace yet strange phenomenon called electricity. Practical use was being made of electricity long before a modern understanding of it was attained, and such an understanding is still based on models of the behavior of particles too small to be seen. Another example is the less common, though well-funded, world of quantum physics. In this arcane area of investigation, mysterious particles (that can also be waves) are identified and described mathematically, but this phenomenon is not truly understood. Unanswered questions are found in all the other sciences, though there is always a belief (and usually plenty of funding) that eventually such mysteries will be solved. Perhaps the best way to deal with the question of a scientific explanation for how astrology works is to suggest that there may be an acceptable one in the future, but we are without one for the present.

A number of theories have been forwarded concerning the nature of the link between terrestrial life and the Sun, Moon, and planets. For many years, physical cause-and-effect theories of astrology have drawn attention to the gravitational effects of the Moon and its obvious links to tides and biological cycles in marine organisms. Some serious studies, as well as the personal experiences of nurses and policemen, suggest a link between the phases of the Moon and crime rates, hemorrhaging, and other sorts of crises. While the Moon, and to a much lesser extent, the Sun, exert a measurable gravitational effect on Earth, that of the other planets is extremely small. Since all the planets are used in astrology, perhaps gravity is only a partial explanation for the astrological effect.

Other physical theories have been forwarded to explain how planets could affect a person. John Nelson, a solar-storm forecaster for RCA, found that specific angular separations between the planets coincided with solar disturbances and consequent magnetic field disruptions on Earth. Astronomer

Percy Seymour proposed that the planets, through their gravitational forces, modulate solar activity and these changes are transmitted to Earth where they affect the magnetic field. It is true that the nervous systems of humans and other animals have electromagnetic properties; perhaps life on Earth is affected by subtle changes in Earth's magnetic field. It is apparent to many astrologers that planets moving slowly seem to have a greater effect than those moving rapidly. Pluto, a dwarf planet that moves very slowly from the perspective of Earth, seems to have an extremely potent astrological effect. Mercury normally moves very quickly, but when it reaches a part of its orbit relative to Earth where it appears to slow down, its effects become stronger. It may be that the longer a planet occupies a specific position, the stronger is its effect on Earth's magnetic field or perhaps the human body itself. It has been found that amniotic fluid has electrical properties and some have suggested that only at birth is the brain fully exposed, and imprinted, to Earth's electromagnetic field pattern.

Other theories suggest that a preoccupation with a physical cause-and-effect linkage may be misleading and that perhaps the nature of life is far more complex than most scientists suspect. Although most astrology books, including this one, focus primarily on the astrology of human life, this is only one of many applications that astrology has to offer. Any astrologer will tell you that charts made for events, such as the opening of a business, a marriage, or a launch, work quite well. Charts calculated for the time that the Sun is exactly at the equinoxes or solstices are often used for weather forecasting. These are charts for supposedly inanimate processes – but how inanimate are they? By accepting the fact that astrology works, we are challenged to question assumptions about the way the world and human consciousness operates. Astrology opens up a vista into the nature of our existence that is mind-boggling, to say the least.

Some astrologers have found that psychologist Carl Jung's ideas on the human psyche, archetypes and synchronicity provide a possible explanation. From Jung's point of view the planets embody deep forms, the archetypes, that are accessed by the human psyche. In this sense the astrological effect is non-causal; humanity and the planets are only parts of a much larger cosmic psychic process. Jung used the idea of synchronicity to explain things like simultaneous discoveries and other strange coincidences. Two events happening at the same time (for example, an alignment of Mars and Venus and the arousal of passionate love) may not necessarily be directly connected, but may be indirectly unified because both are part of a larger cosmic process. In this view, Earth is the microcosm that is affected by the macrocosm within which it exists.

Popular scientific metaphysical thinking has become more wide-ranging in recent years. We've seen a number of books published that draw parallels between the strange world of particle physics and the occult philosophies of eastern religions, which in many ways are supportive of astrology. Rupert Sheldrake's theory of formative causation is suggestive of non-material forms that shape organisms and their behaviors. One perspective that has been developing for a century or more is system science, a scientific approach to nature that is holistic. System science, a broad category that includes cybernetics, chaos theory and fractals, investigates self-organizing systems. Examples of self-organizing systems, where something new and unpredictable emerges from the interaction patterns of many parts, include storms like hurricanes and tornados, the behavior of a flock of birds or a human mob, and life itself from a single cell to a complex organism. In a self-organizing system, the whole is more than the sum of the parts, which is what makes these phenomena so difficult to study with modern science that breaks nature into parts and studies them in isolation. In other writings I have pointed out that the subject matter of astrological analysis is self-organizing systems, and that any understanding of astrology itself must consider the systems perspective.[5]

---

5 See B. Scofield. Astrology as an analytical technique for the study of self-organized systems. *Syzygy*, vol. 9. 2019-2020.

My definition of astrology is this; *astrology is the subject that measures and maps the trajectories of self-organizing systems.* The solar system is the higher-level system within which the Earth system and its inhabitants exist, a situation not unlike that of an organ that controls the cells of which it is made, or a body that controls its organs. Astrology then maps the larger system (solar system) and applies this information to the systems that function within it. Systems that astrology has historically addressed include the body, the personality, group consciousness, the stock market, the weather and the Earth system itself. It follows that because self-organizing systems themselves are notoriously hard to pin down with traditional reductionistic scientific methodologies that look only at the parts, astrology, which maps systems, not parts, would also be difficult to explain. For the present, one can only say that much work needs to be done before this persistent question of exactly how astrology works can be answered with certainty.

Astrology and Religion

People who are unfamiliar with astrology have sometimes regarded it as a religion. While it is true that the gods for which the planets were named were worshiped in ancient times, astrology itself has always been a study and a practical body of knowledge, not a ritual based on faith. The monotheistic religions of the Western world, in their quest for uniformity of belief, have been suspicious of astrology which they believe negates doctrines of free-will. It is true that if astrology was fatalistic (astrologers don't think it is) this would imply a lesser role for God or the priesthood in a person's life. The clergy has also reacted negatively when astrologers have charted the rise and fall of religions or calculated a birth chart for Jesus. The more tolerant religions of the East have not had such a problematic relationship with the subject, and some have even incorporated astrology into their programs for spiritual enlightenment.

In the Bible, astrology is represented in both positive and negative ways. In Genesis, God creates the Sun and Moon as signs in the sky, and also a means to determine the seasons, days, and years. In Matthew (2), it is the astrologers (magi) who are first on the scene in recognizing the importance of the birth of Christ. They also hear the word of God and refuse to cooperate with Herod. Religious leaders who attack astrology usually use biblical quotations out of context to support their arguments. For example, in Isaiah (47) and Daniel (2-5), it is the astrologers of the ancient Near East, not astrology itself, that are attacked as being incompetent, misguided, and inferior to Daniel, God's master dream-interpreter and psychic.

Religious skeptics generally fail to make any distinctions between astrology and practices such as witchcraft, fortune-telling, serpent charming, or necromancy. This is unfortunate and only continues a long tradition of ignorance and misunderstanding of the true nature of the subject. There is nothing in astrology that repudiates religion, and most astrologers have strong spiritual inclinations or practice one of the major religions. It could be said, however, that knowledge of astrology leads one to a view of life that is not exclusive to one religion, but also inclusive of many alternative forms of spirituality.

Conclusion

Hopefully, this brief outline will help to compensate for the lack of factual information available to the public. Online and magazine "horoscopes" are assumed by many to be all that astrology has to offer. But Sun-sign horoscope columns are about as representative of astrology as the Dear Abby advice columns are of psychology. Most people are prejudiced against astrology because they have been programmed by the media to view it as entertainment. It never occurs to them that there is a vast body of serious writing and research on the subject available online and in libraries and bookstores. Those who regard astrology as superstition or self-deception know virtually nothing about it. Certain popular science writers scoff at astrology but make no effort to inform themselves as to its subtleties. When those who have the podium (i.e. the scientists, academicians, politicians, and clergy) reject astrology out of hand, the average person, who is prone to let others do his thinking for him, is apt to do the same. In this hostile cultural environment, progress in researching and improving astrology is made very difficult, yet somehow astrology has survived.

2

What Astrologers Do

Traditionally, astrology has been divided into two primary branches originally called universal and genethliacal astrology. By the Renaissance universal astrology came to be called natural astrology, a category that includes applications to natural phenomena such as weather, agriculture, earthquakes, plagues and also the affairs of cities and states and their politics and economics. Genethliacal astrology was concerned with the character and destiny of individuals. During the Renaissance this branch was called judicial astrology and included the astrology of questions and right-timing. Judicial astrology, because it worked closely with the concerns of individuals, was seen by the religious enemies of astrology as dangerous because it was thought to interfere with free-will. The astrologers saw it as enhancing free-will, however. Today genethliacal astrology is called natal astrology and is by far the most widely practiced branch of astrology.

Natural Astrology
Agricultural astrology is ancient and is concerned with the cycles of the seasons which clearly follow the motions of the Sun. Other planetary factors are considered in regard to determining years of good and bad harvest and the possibility of plagues. The cycles of the Moon are most important in regard to the breeding and gestation cycles of domesticated animals. Agricultural astrology has been kept alive for centuries by Farmer's almanacs which contain tables of astronomical and astrological data.

Astrometeorology is the study of correlations between planetary configurations and the weather. This branch also dates back to the origins of astrology and is still practiced today. The weather forecasts in popular almanacs were, and often still are today, based on astrometeorology. There is now scientific research that supports some astrometeorological principles.[6]

Mundane astrology concerns itself with historical and political trends. This includes predictions of changes in government, election forecasts, market behaviors, wars, or the astrological analysis of a nation's history. Mundane astrology was the earliest known type of astrology, practiced at least 4,000 years ago by astrologers in ancient Mesopotamia.

Judicial Astrology

Natal astrology is concerned with the life patterns of individuals. Using a chart calculated for the time, date and place of birth, an assessment of potentials is determined and this is combined with ongoing planetary activity in order to make estimates of future conditions.

Horary astrology, which means the "astrology of the hour," is a technique that is used to answer questions with a chart calculated for the time the question was asked. This branch of astrology, which does not require an individual's exact birth time, was widely practiced during the Renaissance. It is still used by many of today's practitioners of natal astrology.

Electional astrology is concerned with computing in advance the best time to take important actions such as opening a business or getting married. In the past, merchants relied greatly on this technique, and ships were launched for the first time, or set sail for distant ports, at precise times set by astrologers.

Medical astrology is concerned with the analysis of disease through astrological symbolism. It was used in ancient times by Hippocrates and Galen, and later by many other physicians including Nicolas Culpepper, famous for his book on herbs. One common technique used by medical astrologers of the past was to calculate a astrological chart for the time that

---

6   (for example, see *Science* (1962), Vol. 137, pp. 748-750).

the patient became ill and took to bed, or was injured. An analysis of such a chart gave the practitioner insights into what might be the best treatment for the patient and when critical periods would occur. In earlier times and during the Renaissance, medical practitioners frequently relied on herbs for cures. Each herb was linked to a specific astrological symbol.

The Astrological Chart

Astrologers derive information about a person or an event from a map of the sky calculated for a specific time, date and place. This map, very much like a photograph or time-slice of the sky, is the standard astrological chart, sometimes called the horoscope.[7] From the positions of the Sun, Moon, and planets at the time, date and place of birth, the practitioner of natal astrology attempts to analyze the basic nature and pre-disposition of an individual and forecast future life trends. There are other methodologies used by astrologers, however, including graphs and various kinds of data tables.

As in other fields of study, individual practitioners vary in the techniques they use. Some astrologers include the positions of certain asteroids, some add hypothetical bodies, some use stars, quasars, and even the galactic center. All these positions are calculated from precise astronomical tables for the exact time, date and place of an event or a person's birth. The resulting information is usually noted on a circular chart, the astrological chart, which is a map of the sky at the moment and location of a critical transition point. The astrological chart itself is the primary data source for interpretation, but additional detailed astronomical information derived from the birth chart is often listed on separate pages.

The position of the Sun, Moon, or a planet at the date, time and place of birth are facts that all astrologers must accept as the basis of any interpretation. Only a miscalculation accounts for any real differences in the construction of

---

7   Horoscope is Greek for "hour view" so it actually refers to the Ascendant, not the entire astrological chart.

an astrological chart. There can, however, be minor differences which are due to variations in method, such as the following. Although most astrologers today use the tropical zodiac (mentioned in Chapter 1), some (including Hindu astrologers) use the sidereal zodiac. While this does not alter the relationships between the planets and the horizon, it often changes the sign that they are located in. Practicing astrologers must also choose which house system they will use in their work. (The house systems are methods of dividing the sky and are discussed in Chapter 8.) There is no universally agreed-upon house system, and sometimes a planet's house position in one system will change in another system. Procedural differences such as these are also common in other disciples, notably psychology and medicine.

In the past astrologers had to compute the positions of the planets by hand using trigonometry, a process that could take many hours. Today, most professional astrologers use computer software which frees them from those laborious but necessary mathematical calculations. In a matter of seconds, modern astrological software can produce data for interpretation that would have taken days to compute not that long ago. One benefit of astrological software is that it allows astrologers to experiment with a variety of techniques, some of which are very difficult to calculate by hand. In time, it is possible that a consensus may arise as to which ones work more consistently.

Interpreting the astrological chart

The real difference among astrologers lies in the way the data is interpreted. As in other interpretive fields like medicine and psychology, it is the practitioner's individual skills that count most. In interpreting a birth chart, the astrologer uses the planets as a set of symbols that are uniquely arranged at every birth. Each planet is said to symbolize a specific psychological urge. For example, Mars symbolizes assertiveness and competitiveness. If Mars were rising at the time and place of a birth, most astrologers would agree that the assertive qualities of that individual would be prominent, resulting most often in a bold, competitive, and possibly combative personality. (Gauquelin's study showed that more elite athletes were born with Mars rising.)

To the competent astrologer, astrological symbols in a birth chart can reveal many things: an individual's early life experiences, inherited predispositions, and basic life challenges. Essentially, the astrologer seeks to understand a person's potential and, in a positive sense, can often bring into focus hidden strengths and talents. The astrologer offers to individuals an account of who they are, where they have been, and where they might go in order to realize their potential. Unlike the psychologist, the astrologer can reach such conclusions rapidly, even without ever having met the client.

The technical skills of astrological chart interpretation do not necessarily guarantee that every astrological practitioner will have excellent social skills. The best practicing astrologers are also expert counselors and consultants with extensive experience and a solid knowledge of human nature. They must be able to use computers and handle mathematical problems, understand psychological terminology and theory, and be able to counsel people who may be going through difficult times in their lives. In addition they must be able to manage their own business, advertising and promotion. These are not ordinary qualifications and being a practicing astrologer is not an easy job.

Forecasting with Astrology

Probably the most controversial, intriguing, and popular aspect of astrology has to do with the prediction of the future. Strictly speaking, predicting an exact event in the future is impossible. What the astrologer can do is forecast the nature of trends and locate points in time when physical, social, or psychological events may occur. Astrologers find that, while the timing of an event or trend is reliably predictable, a person's response to the event is not. While the timing of specific circumstances appears to be fated (or pre-programmed), our free-will can color the nature and quality of our responses.

What Astrology is ...And How to Use it

There is nothing inherently mystical in astrological forecasting, as you will see in the following example. The first necessity is a listing of the positions of the planets for each day, this being found online or in book form, known as an ephemeris. Using these tables (or a computer), the astrologer is able to calculate astrological charts showing the positions of the Sun, Moon, and planets in relation to a specific time and place on Earth.

As an example, let us use the birth chart of former President Richard Nixon. At the time of his birth, the Sun was at 19 degrees of Capricorn. This means that for his entire life, Richard Nixon was sensitive to this degree area. The position of the Sun in a birth chart symbolizes a person's physical body, vitality, and personal power, and the sign Capricorn symbolizes profession, honor, and reputation. As you might well imagine, the Sun in Capricorn would be a very important point in the birth chart of a president. In late 1974, the planet Saturn, symbolizing obstacles and problems, was transiting (moving) through the 19th degree of Cancer, exactly opposite the sign and degree of the Sun at Nixon's birth. Astrologers call this alignment "transiting Saturn in opposition to the natal Sun." The transit itself is an astronomical fact, but it is abstract and without meaning until the astrologer calls upon his knowledge of astrological symbolism to make sense of this alignment and offer an interpretation.

Transiting Saturn being opposite Nixon's Sun degree in late 1974 suggests that he would encounter serious obstacles at this time. The accumulated experiences of thousands of astrologers over the past 2,500 years has shown that the opposition of Saturn to the Sun often occurs around the time of important life decisions, often made under pressure. It has also been observed that problems tend to accumulate in a person's life at such a time and frequently a decision is made to separate from something, often a residence, a job, or a marriage. Not every case is the same, but there is a general pattern recognized by astrologers today and historically.

Now, since we know that Nixon's Sun position symbolizes his honor and status, and that Saturn opposite the Sun often symbolizes problems and possible separations, we could make a prediction. We could state that, "in the latter part of 1974, Richard Nixon will face a great challenge to his status and may choose to pull back or separate from his professional life." Interestingly, many astrologers made such a forecast prior to his resignation from the presidency in August, 1974. There is more about astrological forecasting in Chapter 9.

The Philosophy of an Astrologer

While there is no universally accepted philosophy or belief system associated with astrology, one could say that most astrologers think holistically. Frequent confirmation of the idea that the planetary positions correlate with life on Earth leads many astrologers toward a broad outlook and an interest in subjects like cosmology, Eastern religions and consciousness studies. Because astrologers see and experience an inter-connectedness between people, things of the world, events and time, they use their astrological knowledge to work with nature and enhance it, rather than to dominate or control it.

Many astrologers believe in some form of reincarnation, though there is nothing in astrology that makes this belief necessary. During the late 19th and early 20th centuries, a number of prominent astrologers were associated with the Theosophical Society, a group that embraces reincarnation. Many who learned from these astrologers have assumed a close linkage between the two. Reincarnation is, however, a belief that may be held by people in any walk of life. It is not supported any more by astrology than it is by psychology.

What Makes a Good Astrologer?

Astrologers may be self-taught or study under a teacher, and after years of practice, emerge as respected professionals. Some astrologers learn and practice only one type of astrology, while others are more versatile. Unlike medicine and law, astrology today has no universally accepted standards though there are a few certification programs offered by astrological organizations and schools of astrology. See Appendix D for a list of astrology schools around the world.

Merely passing a difficult test, however, is no guarantee that someone is competent. Some doctors and lawyers have passed licensing tests, yet they are still not fit to practice. Also, astrologers are capable of explaining through astrology only what they are capable of understanding. A good astrologer needs good knowledge of human nature. A degree in social work, psychology or one of the other social sciences can be useful in this regard. Ultimately the practice of astrology is interpretive and diagnostic, and proficiency comes with experience. Like the best doctors, the best astrologers are those who have perfected their judgment over a long period of time. For information on astrological readings and what you could expect from one, see Appendix A.

3

The History of Astrology

Since ancient times, agricultural communities have relied on knowledge of the changes of the seasons and the fertility cycles of animals. Observing the movements of the Sun and Moon and their correlations with these crucial biological rhythms led to the development of the first sciences which were essential for civilization and an orderly community life – astronomy, astrology and calendrics.

Early humans lived close to nature. They noticed that the point in the east where the Sun rises every day changes throughout the year, and that this movement coincides with both the changes of the seasons and the lengths of day and night. They saw that the cycle of the Moon from new to full was linked to mammalian fertility cycles. They built calendar sites and temples aligned to the points on the horizon where these regular astronomical phenomena occurred to keep calendars accurate. Pyramids and temples in Egypt and Mexico, as well as stone circles like Stonehenge in the British Isles, have survived from ancient times, testifying to the importance of skywatching in the development of civilization.

As civilization progressed, the phases of the Moon, eclipses, and the cycles of the planets were recorded and compared with events on Earth. Floods, political changes, wars, economic fluctuations, and events in people's lives were correlated with activity in the sky. Over the years, certain patterns and relationships became apparent. Correlations between the movements of the Sun, Moon, and planets with human life, animals, plants and weather was obvious to humanity worldwide. These empirical correlations became the basis for the astrology practiced today. Eventually, astrology, astronomy, and calendar science developed as a single body of knowledge that studied humanity's relationship to the astronomical cycles and people made practical use of this knowledge.

Although religious significance was often attached to the planets and to particular days in the yearly cycle (as it still is today), astrology was not, in itself, a religion. It was a system of knowledge based on accumulated observations, and it gave early humanity some sense of security and order in an otherwise unpredictable world. Astrology and astronomy were considered to be one and the same subject in Roman times through the Middle Ages. Only during the late Renaissance did they separate.

Ancient Mesopotamia

Relationships between humans and their celestial environment were noted throughout the world wherever civilization developed. But it was in ancient Mesopotamia, a region of acute natural and political instability, that this activity reached its zenith. Here, astronomical and atmospheric phenomena were observed, carefully recorded, and interpreted for the ruling elite by astronomer-priests. This may have begun with the Sumerians, perhaps the oldest civilization in the Near East, but it was sustained and developed by the Akkadians, Assyrians, Babylonians, and other civilizations that flourished in the region up to the age of the Romans. Detailed observations were made more or less continuously for several thousand years. Ultimately, astrology in Mesopotamia became a highly sophisticated omen system based on rigorous astronomical observations and the accumulated experience of generations of sky interpreters. It influenced religion, philosophy, government, and politics. Our seven-day week, each day of which is named for a planet, is an astrological remnant of ancient Near Eastern sky-consciousness.

India, China and Mesoamerica

Astrology also developed elsewhere. In India, an ancient native astrology blended with Greco-Mesopotamian astrology to produce a unique system still practiced today. Astrology has always been popular in India, and it has not suffered the discrediting it has experienced in most Western cultures. There are astrological colleges in India and the subject is employed at the highest levels of government.

In China, astrologers favored a polar-based system of measurement, in contrast to the Mesopotamian measuring system which was based on the Sun's path or ecliptic. The Chinese, as well as the Indians, also used a twenty-eight-sign zodiac, based on the motion of the Moon. The popular 12-year cycle of animals in Chinese astrology is only one part of a more complex system based around cycles of 12 and 10 that has an ancient pedigree. Traditional Chinese astrology is still practiced in China but is not well-known in the West.

At the time of the Spanish Conquest, Mesoamerica (Mexico and northern Central America) was at least as culturally advanced as ancient Mesopotamia, India, and China. It also had a form of astrology, a unique form that emphasized time. (In the West, sky events were measured spatially; in Mexico, time itself acted like a zodiacal sign.) The ancient Maya, Toltec, and Aztec astrologers used a sequence of 20 days that acted like zodiacal signs and which repeated endlessly, much like our 7-day week. These 20 day-signs cycled with 13 sacred numbers, producing an astrological calendar of 260 days, a figure that meshes with several planetary periodicities. Other astronomical cycles, ranging from days to millennia, were part of this astrological system. The ancient Mesoamericans also held the planet Venus in high regard and made predictions based on its movements.

While the indigenous Hindu, Chinese, and Mesoamerican astrological systems were quite sophisticated and held potential for further development, the astrology practiced today throughout the Western world is rooted in the astrology of ancient Mesopotamia.

Ancient Greece
During the centuries before and after Alexander's conquest of the Near East, there was contact between Greece and Mesopotamia which led to

significant developments in astrology. An emphasis on the distance between planets as seen from Earth led to the doctrine of aspects which measure the phases of a cycle. It was during this period that the 12-sign zodiac, which had been developing for hundreds of years, became a major feature. It was probably Greek natural philosophers who arranged the various components of Mesopotamian astrology into a system structured by spatial geometry.

The notion of a map of the sky calculated for the time and place of a person's birth was probably the most important development during this period. Originally, Mesopotamian astrology had concerned itself mainly with the life of the nation or kingdom. The king was the center of the human world and only the planets at his birth were considered worth examining. But the oldest surviving astrological chart (410 B.C.) was made for a commoner. The Greeks, who placed a high value on the individual, stimulated the transition in astrology from a study of the king and the kingdom to the study of individual lives.

Ancient Rome

When Rome became the dominant Mediterranean power, astrology gained in prestige and influence. Astrologers were often the most learned men of their times, and most emperors relied on their advice. At least two emperors, Tiberius and Hadrian, were practicing astrologers themselves. There were plenty of public practitioners as well. Astrology was supported by Stoicism, a philosophy popular with many leading Romans. At certain times, astrological predictions of the deaths of famous people became so excessive that mass expulsions of astrologers were ordered and laws were passed to regulate the practice of astrology. During the Roman Empire, many books on astrology were written, several of which survive. The most famous, the *Tetrabiblos* of Claudius Ptolemy, was written around A.D. 150 and became the major handbook of astrology during the Middle Ages and Renaissance. The techniques of Roman astrologers were very sophisticated, and many are still used today or have served to stimulate new developments in the field.

The History of Astrology

Until recently, only a small portion of the many surviving Greek and Roman astrological writings were translated into English. Also, most translations were done by scholars hostile to astrology. To remedy this situation, Project Hindsight was founded in 1992 to reclaim astrology's ancient roots. Funded entirely by the astrological community, several astrologically-minded translators produced translations of important and valuable ancient astrological writings. These opened up some new perspectives on the subject which stimulated lively discussions within the field. Today there are many who study and practice what's known as Hellenistic or Classical astrology.

After the Fall of Rome
While Europe was in the Dark Ages, the Islamic world became the bright light of Western civilization. The scientific works of the Greeks and Romans had suffered at the hands of barbarians and religious fanatics, but in intellectual centers like Baghdad and in Moslem Spain those that survived were copied and recopied. Arab scientists also made some significant advances in the field, particularly in regard to cycles of planetary conjunctions, weather and derived points called Arabic Parts. In order to avoid potential religious conflicts, Arabic astrology focused on historical and political astrology rather than on human births. During the 12th and 13th centuries, Arab manuscripts began to circulate in Europe. This influx of information brought about a revival of astrology, accompanied by Christian rationalizations for its existence by leading scholars and theologians including Albertus Magnus, Thomas Aquinas and Roger Bacon. Within a few centuries astrology was being taught in the universities, and most Italian courts included an astrologer.

In the 14th century came the Black Death, a devastating plague that cut Europe's population by perhaps 50% or more. This event, which caused the deaths of many religious officials, weakened the power of the Church as it raised questions about God's plans and the ability of the clergy to interpret what they might be. Astrologers pointed to suspicious planetary alignments as the cause of corrupted Air that was thought to cause the plague and these explanations were taken seriously. This situation left the Church in a weakened position culturally and left astrology free to pursue its objects of study and provide information to those who wanted it. By the 15th century, astrology had regained the social position it had held in ancient times. It was practiced by the most learned men, used by leaders for decision-making, and served as a model for understanding the cosmos and the planets roles in a person's life. Up until the 16th and 17th centuries in the West, astrology and astronomy were usually practiced by the same person. After this, they became separated and astrology experienced another decline. The reasons for this are complex and will be examined in Chapter 4.

The Renaissance and the fate of astrology

By the early sixteenth century in Europe, astrology was being taught in the universities and practiced in the courts of kings. But at the end of this century, its prestige had declined considerably. It could be said that the decline of astrology began in 1497 when a book that attacked astrology by Pico della Mirandola, the great humanist and religious fanatic, was published. In *Disputationes adversus astrologiam divinatricem (trans*lated as *Disputations Against Divinatory Astrology* or sometimes as just *Against the Astrologers)* Pico argued that astrology should be rejected because it denied free-will to humans and power to God. In his view, humans were self-contained beings having the power to improve themselves. "If this is so," he argued, "how can humans be controlled by the planets?" Pico saw God as the ultimate power who would send angels to help men on special occasions. Prayer would not be so important if astrology was legitimized. He argued that God certainly wouldn't use the planets as agents of His will, therefore the planets could also have no real effects on people. In his attack on astrology, Pico selected information that supported his arguments but he suppressed any to the contrary. Pico could have been accused of twisting the facts, but to those who knew nothing about astrology, he seemed to be speaking the truth with intense passion and appeal to religious beliefs.

Pico's attack on astrology had all the conviction and supreme confidence of a religious fanatic. Another reason for his rage was that certain astrologers had predicted he would die early in life – and he did. But even more important for our concern is the fact that his book became an encyclopedia of arguments against astrology that were used by other objectors. Many other works were written against astrology over the next two hundred years, and much of the material was taken directly from Pico. Most of these attacks on astrology were for religious reasons and centered on the issue of free-will.

The Reformation

From about 1520 onwards, religious passions were aroused all over Europe which led to educational, political, and economic changes. Religious wars and conflicts drew everyone's attention. Religious reforms, initiated by powerful men like Luther and Calvin, emphasized the importance of the individual and his relationship to God, not the planets or stars. In a world of uncertainty, death, and famine, people sought explanations which both astrologer and priest were able to provide. Religious leaders therefore saw astrology as serious competition. For the next 150 years, the clergy attacked astrology with a vengeance. Overall, the astrologers were more flexible and inclusive. They could believe in God, be Christians, and still practice their art, which they argued was created by God in the first place. They stated that "the stars incline, they do not compel," and that therefore free-will existed – astrology gave people knowledge that could be used to make informed choices. They also pointed out that, according to the Bible, God had put signs in the heavens for humankind to see and use. Nevertheless, religion was no friend to astrology and the clergy continued their attacks. Even more than the Scientific Revolution, the war on astrology from religion damaged astrology so severely that it has barely survived and is only now beginning to recover.

The Loss of Royal Patronage

During the Middle Ages, astrologers had held relatively secure positions as private consultants to kings and nobility. But as the fabric of the provincial medieval world was torn apart and the commercially-oriented world of the Renaissance came into being, astrologers were freed from their supporting ties to a single patron.

The printing press created the possibility of serving a greater audience, and this led to annual astrological almanacs being published, the predecessors of some still in print today. Astrologers found themselves competing with one another for popularity. They made predictions for every major planetary configuration, and each astrologer claimed to be more accurate than others. As would be expected, the most outrageous and vocal astrologers were heard widely and the more cautious were not. For example, in February 1524, all the visible planets were grouped in the sign Pisces. Several years before this event, predictions of a great flood began to appear, and competing astrologers hurled insults at each other. The more sober astrologers did not predict a flood, but they were overshadowed by the drama of the more extreme predictions. Though it was an unusually wet year, the predicted flood did not occur, and astrologers in general suffered discredit in the eyes of the public and were deemed a public menace by leaders and government.

By the mid-17th century the practice of astrology had changed dramatically. Most full-time astrologers were peddling their services in big cities or were publishing almanacs. Some, like the great astrologer William Lilly of London, were very successful and even consulted by royalty and members of Parliament. But in an age where few people knew their birth times, most of the astrology practiced was horary astrology (answering questions using a chart cast for the time that the client poses the query). More like a form of divination than an exact science, horary astrology was even more out of step than natal astrology with the big happenings in the newly emerging scientific community. The new science of astronomy and the practice of astrology had begun to part ways.

The Split Between Astrology and Astronomy

For fifteen hundred years, astrology had been supported by the theories of Ptolemy and Aristotle. Ptolemy had said that the Earth lay at the center of the universe, and the planets orbited the Earth in complex cycles. In 1543, Nicolas Copernicus published a manuscript suggesting that the Sun, not the Earth, was at the center. While Ptolemy's model could actually predict a planet's future position with some degree of accuracy, Copernicus' model, especially when it was improved by Johannes Kepler, worked better and it became gradually more accepted as the best model. When Ptolemy's astronomical theory was rejected, his astrology became questionable.

The same thing happened to Aristotle's teachings, partly because of discoveries made by Tycho Brahe. Tycho was a Danish astrologer who, upon finding glaring errors in the planetary tables of his day, devoted his life to making accurate measurements of the planets and stars. He was interested in astrology early in life and consistently defended it, maintaining that accurate astrological analysis was not possible without accurate observation of the heavens. He acquired the patronage of the Danish king, who consulted him on astrological matters such as his sons' astrological charts. Tycho also made accurate predictions regarding the weather and political changes. Today, Tycho is regarded as the founder of modern observational astronomy; science books fail to stress his original astrological motivations.

Tycho was one of the first to report on the New Star of 1572, a supernova that appeared suddenly and lasted for over a year. Tycho's meticulous observations led him to conclude that the new star was located in what was previously considered the unchanging sphere of the fixed stars. Later, in 1577, he noted that a comet had cut through what people believed were solid crystalline spheres of the separate heavens. Ancient authorities had declared that such things were impossible. Aristotle had postulated a series of heavens above the Earth with forces emanating from the highest to the lowest. This notion, which had provided a theory of how the planets and stars could influence earthly life, became unacceptable when Tycho's discoveries about the supernova and comet proved that Aristotle's model of the universe was wrong. Theories that had for centuries made astrology seem rational to intellectuals were now being discredited. Worse yet, the discrediting of Ptolemy and Aristotle was being led by the most scientific astrologers of the time.

Traditional notions of the nature of the heavens were further upset by the appearance of another supernova in 1604 and by Galileo's discovery of the moons orbiting Jupiter in 1609. Trained only to read astrological charts, most astrologers were unprepared to offer theoretical explanations. Only those who had strong technical interests (like Tycho) could address these problems. At this time the scientific method, initiated by Francis Bacon, Descartes and others was becoming the major trend in intellectual circles. Perhaps the most crucial problem for astrology and astrologers during this time was in regard to making it into a science. This was an impossible task because astrology as a practice was interpretive and concerned with probabilities. Except for the motions of the planets there were no consistent units in an astrological analysis that could be measured and placed in a mathematical equation.

Following up on Tycho's work was Johannes Kepler, the first to mathematically describe the solar system as we know it today. But Kepler was also an accomplished astrologer who made some very accurate weather predictions and political forecasts. It was Kepler who, in response to the critics of astrology, said "don't throw out the baby with the bath water." He knew that astrology should be updated but, like Tycho, put most of his energy into solving the great astronomical problems of his time. What few people know is that even while Kepler's work made Copernicus' theory a scientific truth, he was guided by astrological ideas. For example, he developed a theory of the harmonies formed by the orbital velocities of the planets, part of his attempt to compose a grand synthesis of mathematics, music, astronomy, and astrology – a theory of everything.

By the 17th century, the traditional position of the astrologer in society had changed dramatically. The measurement of the heavens had become a separate discipline called astronomy. Kepler had suggested that astrology be reformed, but his reforms were too extreme for most astrologers to accept. He advocated abandoning the zodiac, except as a convenient reference, and placed nearly all his emphasis on the aspects or angles between the planets. Interestingly, Kepler's ideas on astrology have had some impact in the 20th century, particularly on the German schools of Cosmobiology and Uranian astrology, and also on English astrologer John Addey's theory of harmonics.

Other 17th-century astrologers tried to make a science out of astrology. In a large treatise on astrometeorology, John Goad correlated the aspects of the planets with the weather in London, Germany, and other parts of the world. He kept a weather diary for thirty years, and attempted to show that a specific weather pattern frequently occurred at the same time as a particular planetary aspect.[8] Unfortunately, modern statistical techniques for analyzing such data were not to be developed for nearly 150 years and his work did not meet up to the standards of the new experimental science. The intellectual climate was changing rapidly in the 17th century. Astronomers abandoned the theories and techniques of astrology and astrologers failed in their attempts to be a part of the Scientific Revolution.

The Rise of Modern Science

The great movement of the 17th century was the rise of modern science, especially in physics. Its founders (then called natural philosophers) were pursuing entirely different problems than their medieval forebears. They wanted to measure material things precisely with mathematics, and they wanted to make flawless predictions. To do so, they found it necessary to limit their studies to astronomical, physical, mechanical, and engineering problems. The kind of science they developed is called reductionist and is concerned analyzing parts taken into the laboratory – the whole is the sum of the parts. This kind of science is also materialist (all is matter), mechanistic

---

8   Scofield, B. A signal from Saturn found in daily temperature data. *Correlation*. 29 (1), 52-65, 2013.

(everything is machine-like, including life) and deterministic (everything has a traceable cause or is a cause). Problems of a human or psychological nature, which astrology had addressed, could not be measured with mathematics, so these were either left to the clergy or ignored.

In the latter part of the 17th century, the major figure in this changing intellectual and scientific mainstream was the mathematician and physicist Isaac Newton. He was the greatest scientist of his time and had a tremendous influence on intellectuals then and for many years afterward – and he wasn't interested in astrology.[9] What was truly unique about Newton was that he stamped an entirely new philosophy of nature on the Western consciousness. With his brilliant mathematical solutions to problems of motion (which were based on Kepler's work), Newton essentially validated the argument that the universe was nothing but one big machine, a clockwork universe. He, and others of his period, ceased to ask "why" certain phenomena in nature occurred – they were only concerned with "how". Although Newton's treatment of gravity is now regarded as his greatest achievement, he could only measure it, observe it, and make accurate predictions about it; he couldn't say exactly what gravity was. The implications of this approach led to the notion that if something couldn't be measured, then it had no place in physical science. In a sense, mathematical equations became explanations. Taken further, this approach suggests the idea that nature is there to be measured, controlled and dominated, and that humans are separate from nature and its rhythms. Today we are seeing that the fruits of this approach in the form of modern technologies that have been both a blessing and a curse. While human life has been made safer, the natural and biological environment is paying the costs for this advance.

Newton's role in history (and it was a large one) was to bring into focus a major ideological shift. In the new science, astrology had no place because it couldn't be proven, measured, or manipulated. It was simply not an

---

9   Newton was deeply interested in alchemy, however, and wrote on it extensively.

experimental science like physics because it had no units to measure. It was an observational and descriptive study born during a time in history when humanity was seen to be a part of the cycles of nature. Astrology, which carried much ancient baggage in its symbolic methods of interpretation, was incompatible in many respects with the newly emerging science, and it fell out of favor with natural philosophers, later called scientists.

In fairness to astrology, it should be pointed out that if the social sciences, psychology, anthropology, and sociology, had been around during Newton's time (they weren't to be for another two hundred years), they would likely also have been rejected as candidates for the new science, in part because some of their subject material intrudes on the domain of the Church. Today it is mostly statistical analysis that gives scientific credence to the social sciences and in the late 17th century, statistical analysis was still a long way off.

Other Factors in the Decline

Late in the 17th century came more blows to astrology's formerly great prestige. Life in this age was precarious and the clergy had their own explanations for human disasters. They allowed no room for astrology's answers and they took deliberate measures to discredit it. Weakened by their changing socio-economic situation and divided by disagreements on technical matters, astrologers could no longer counter the power of the clergy. Also, the rise of insurance companies, fire companies, and other securities of modern life served to lessen fears of an uncertain future. Astrology became less important when an astrological consultation could be replaced by financial or other arrangements to survive a disaster.

By the 18th century, interest in astrology was no longer found in the higher classes. Just about the only astrology left was found in the popular almanacs, and even these were being attacked in satirical almanacs by writers like Jonathan Swift. Though still a vital part of rural and seafaring life, astrology had gone underground in most cities in Europe by 1750. Astrology did survive as a middle class practice in England, however, for a longer period than on the continent.

In summary, between about 1500 and 1750, astrology was attacked by the Church, abandoned by the astronomers, and discredited by writers – but it never was actually disproved. Slow to adjust to rapidly changing times, astrology was too fatalistic for the humanists, a threat to organized religion, and a burden to the scientists. Another problem was the failure of astrologers to rally around a common theme, to organize and present a united front. We can't be too harsh on them though, they simply found themselves practicing a complex subject in a rapidly changing world.

Astrology Revived

During the 18th and 19th centuries astrology held a very low profile in Europe and the United States. While farmer's almanacs continued to publish weather predictions based on astrology, and a few practitioners kept the traditional methodologies alive, no real innovations were made. But near the end of the 19th century astrology began to make a comeback, first in England and then the United States. A major driving force in the revival of astrology was Theosophy, a popular spiritual movement that brought to the public a mix of ancient holistic philosophies, primarily Hermeticism, Neoplatonism and Hinduism. These provided a philosophical matrix within which astrology made sense and allowed it to spread widely in middle class culture. By the early 20th century, astrologers like Alan Leo in England and Evangeline Adams in the United States had brought the subject into mainstream popular culture again. Newspaper and magazine columns on astrology brought astrology to the masses while a few celebrities began to consult with astrologers. On a more intellectual level, psychologist Carl Jung and artist and philosopher Dane Rudhyar made attempts to explain astrology in modern terms.

During the 1960s astrology became even more popular, which caused a reaction from scientific skeptics who have continuously fought against it. This hasn't made much of a dent in popular astrology which now has a strong presence in bookstores and on the internet. While astrology has changed in many ways, it retains many of its traditional elements. The chief difference is in its adaptation to our present culture. Most astrologers today practice natal astrology and use psychological knowledge in their interpretations of birth charts. To those who understand its possibilities, astrology has much to contribute to our lives in this modern age. As in the ancient past, astrology integrates humankind with natural cycles and gives meaning to seemingly incomprehensible situations. Astrologers and students of astrology need to better understand its history and let the world know of its great and ancient tradition and its future prospects.

4

The Planets and Other Points

The computation of an astrological chart is basically a math problem in astronomy, but what comes after the calculation is entirely different. To actually "do" astrology requires insight, creativity and experience. Interpreting a birth chart involves an understanding of life, the ability to perceive subtle patterns, and the creative blending of a consistently recurring set of symbols. Every birth chart contains the same symbols, but they are arranged in different combinations so that no two charts are exactly the same. Scientists are uncomfortable with astrology partly because the creative interpretation of symbols is different from working with they are used to – discrete units or numbers. Symbolic interpretation (semiotics) is very close to artistic creativity, a long-accepted, non-logical mental process. It is no coincidence that astrologers are often more than casually involved in the arts or music.

There are four main types of astrological symbols. The first are the planets themselves. They are the players, the moving pieces. The word planet comes from the Greek for wanderer, and for astrological purposes this includes the Sun and Moon. The second type of symbol involves the angular separations or alignments between the planets. These angles are called the aspects and they show how the planets relate or don't relate to each other and what phases they are in relative to each other. The zodiacal signs are a third kind of symbol; they modify the basic planetary natures: the Moon is always the Moon, but it functions differently in Libra than it does in Aries. Finally, the houses show if planets are rising or setting and, as compartments, symbolize the areas of day-to-day life in which the planets express their basic natures.

The birth chart is a map of the sky at the time and place of birth. The symbols it contains describe both the internal and external experiences of a person. Each planet is symbolic of a particular function, just as each part of the body is a part of the whole person. The planets can be interpreted as symbols of specific functions on many levels; the physical, psychological, and social levels of being. In the pages ahead we will see how this is so.

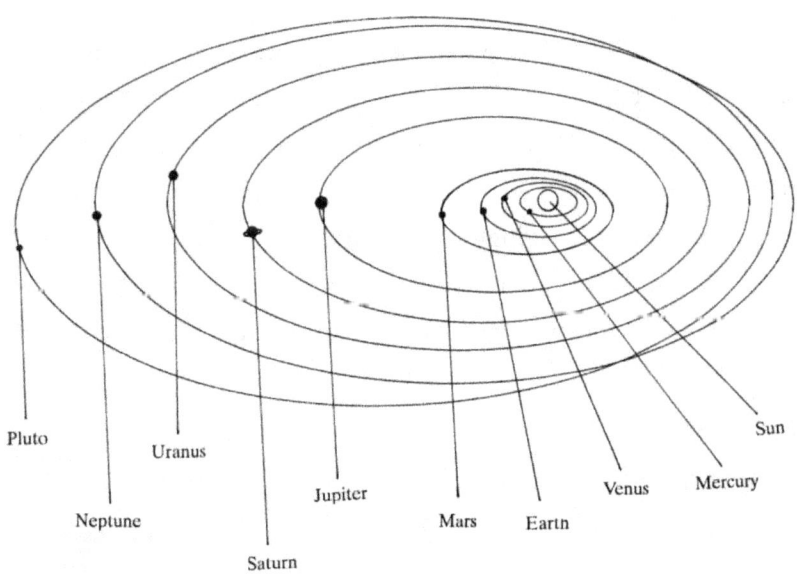

Figure 2. The Astronomy of the Solar System

Planet	Solar Distance	Period	Diameter
Mercury	36,000,000 mi.	88 days	3,010 mi.
Venus	67,270,000 mi.	225 days	7,650 mi.
Earth	92,955,700 mi.	365.25 days	7,900 mi.
Mars	142,000,000 mi.	687 days	4,200 mi.
Jupiter	483,600,000 mi.	11.86 years	85,000 mi.
Saturn	886,700,000 mi.	29.46 years	71,000 mi.
Uranus	1,782,000,000 mi.	84.01 years	31,000 mi.
Neptune	1,794,000,000 mi.	164.8 years	30,000 mi.
Pluto	4,600,000,000 mi.	248.4 years	1,477 mi.

Just as each planet is a part of the entire solar system, in astrology, each planet symbolizes a part of a person's entire being. The discussions that follow here will briefly describe how each planet affects personality, and also what people might be like with that planet emphasized in the birth chart. In these instances, "emphasized" means that the planet holds a position or rulership in the chart that highlights is functions. The most import of these qualifiers is angularity, location near the horizon or the meridian, these two axes being called the angles of the birth chart. As we saw in Chapter 1, the statistical studies of the Gauquelins have demonstrated the strength of planets when they are in such positions.

A second type of emphasis is elevation. The planet in the chart that is highest in its daily arc through the sky will have additional power. This power is highest when the planet is near the Meridian – the Sun is at the meridian once a day at noon.

A third type of emphasis comes via a connection to the sign on the eastern horizon, the rising sign or sign on the Ascendant.[10] Each planet is linked to a sign that has qualities that work with that planet – they resonate. The planet that is linked to, or rules, the rising sign is sometimes called the

---

10   The Ascendant is the term for the degree of the Sun's path that is rising on the eastern horizon. In ancient times this was called the horoscope, a Greek word meaning "view of the hour." The word horoscope has been used improperly for many years, mostly as the name for the entire astrological chart.

ruling planet, though that is technically not always the case. But for our purposes let's call it simply the Ascendant ruler. Wherever it may be located in the chart, it seems to have special significance.

The Luminaries

The Sun is the most dominant of all objects in the sky, and the Moon is the most dominant by night. In traditional astrology these two are often called the Luminaries or the Lights. In an astrological chart, these two bodies symbolize the most basic energies and needs in a person's life.

The Sun

The Sun is a most important point in an astrological chart. While popular Sun-sign astrology attempts to describe people only from the position of the Sun, such interpretation rings true to some extent because of the tremendous power the Sun has in a birth chart. Astrology sees the entire solar system as an analogy for the self; so the Sun, which is a star at the center of our solar system, symbolizes the center of our lives – our vitality and our will to live. As a center of gravity, the Sun holds the solar system together and keeps the planets from flying off into deep space. Just as the physical Sun maintains the integrity of the solar system, the Sun in the birth chart indicates the integrity of the human system. Socially, the Sun is symbolic of the father, authority, and benevolent leadership. In a sense, the Sun is like the captain of a ship who makes choices and steers towards a goal.

Self-worth, self-esteem, and ego-strength are symbolized by the Sun. These qualities are needed for the individual to survive and thrive. The Sun in a birth chart also symbolizes the amount of energy available to the person. A strong Sun, as shown by its sign, house, and aspects, or its position close to the horizon or meridian, indicates both physical and ego-strength and a tendency to dominate the environment in a direct way. People born with an emphasized Sun in their birth-chart are often motivated to exert their power through displays of leadership. A less directly placed Sun does not necessarily mean that the person is weak, it suggests that power and success come through less direct means. Frequently, the person behind the scenes is the real person in charge. A powerfully placed Sun is not necessarily better or more successful than others, it just shows that a great deal of energy is more available to that person and that it is expressed directly. How that energy is managed is what really makes the difference between success and failure.

Natal astrology draws analogies between astrological symbols and parts of the body. Each planet rules the body parts that perform the function that the planet represents. The Sun, associated with vitality and integrity, symbolizes the heart which keeps the body alive, and the spine, which gives it form. Scientific astrobiology teaches that complex Earth life would simply not exist without the Sun, so the symbolism is appropriate.

The Moon

The Moon symbolizes interests, responses, reactions, feelings and instincts. While the Sun is the focal point of the vitality and integrity of the self, the Moon is the focus of the security and nourishment needs. People with an emphasized Moon are typically sensitive, nurturing, and protective. The Moon is also a feminine symbol, specifically the female as mother and prime nurturer. On the most basic levels, satisfaction for the Moon is oral gratification, a need that must be met soon after being born. Immediately after birth, instincts move the infant to seek the security of the mother's breast. The Moon signifies this instinctive need to nourish oneself, and also to form secure attachments. The Moon appears to be a dominant influence during the first two years of life, and corresponds in many respects to Freud's oral stage. Anatomically, the Moon corresponds to the mouth, stomach, breasts, and womb. It also has connections to the sensorium, the general sensory perception of the world.

The Moon is a point in the chart that symbolizes subconscious functioning. It is symbolic of an older portion of the brain which generates actions taken without thought such as instinctive reactions. The Moon represents the pre-verbal mind which is inaccessible to reason – but it does respond to images and threats to security. It is also symbolic of the brain's right hemisphere, the half of the brain that thinks holistically and intuitively. The Moon is thus an important factor in understanding non-rational habits and behaviors.

The position of the Moon in a birth chart shows a person's natural interests and their "instinctive" response to something. (For example, people listen to a particular type of music because there is something in it to which they react.) The Moon also signifies a person's characteristic emotional response. Some people respond to a stimulus dramatically, some tend to suppress their feelings, and others might respond in a creative and balanced manner. It's all shown by the Moon in the birth chart. Continuing the analogy of a ship in which the Sun is the captain, the Moon would be the crew, and also the lookout.

The Inner Planets

In astrology, Mercury, Venus, and Mars are often grouped together as the inner planets. In the solar system they are the rocky planets, close to the Earth and physically small. Venus is almost the same size as the Earth, Mars about half its size and Mercury smaller yet. Along with the Moon, these planets represent functions needed by the individual to cope with life's daily demands. They are considered "personal planets" in that they symbolize important aspects of one's own unique personality.

Mercury
Mercury is symbolic of mental activity and the use of language; it is the planet of thinking and communication. It is linked to the brain's left hemisphere, which is logical, analytical, and literal. The Mercury part of the mind is concerned with knowledge and rational problem-solving, both of which require the ability to use symbols and to manipulate ideas and things. Those

with Mercury emphasized in the birth chart tend to be talkers, readers, writers, and thinkers.

Ancient traditions often associated the planet Mercury with teachers and bringers of knowledge. The Greek god Hermes and the Roman god Mercury were emissaries and messengers. From this perspective, Mercury is the planet that symbolizes the movement of information from one place to another. This movement can also be expressed in other ways. People with an emphasized Mercury often become associated with some form of transportation, either as a career or an interest. Socially, Mercury is symbolic of those who connect others: lawyers, secretaries, agents, messengers, drivers, etc.

On the physical level, Mercury corresponds to the eyes and the nervous system, the networks that move information through the body. A negatively emphasized Mercury can correlate with an overworked nervous system, chronic talking, or smoking. A positively emphasized Mercury often correlates with outstanding speech, productive writing, and some serious walking, running or bicycle riding.

Venus

Venus is the planet of socialization, relationship, love, courtship, and mating. It symbolizes desire and attraction, interactions with others, and the need to get along with them. A person with an emphasized Venus is likely to be very interested in love and partnering, and will probably make key life decisions, both positive and negative, around such issues.

Mate attraction, which requires attention to visual and other sensory information, comes under Venus. Symmetrical proportions are attractive and Venus signifies the need for harmony and balance in art, design and relationships. Venus is thus a refining planet and is symbolic of the human striving for a better life, rather than a return to the animal state. Social harmony, social stability, a sense of equality, and a sense of civilization and culture are all linked to Venus. The position of Venus in the birth chart also shows what a person values – in art, music and other people. Venus is traditionally a feminine symbol. While the Moon is the mother, Venus depicts the beautiful and sexually desirable aspect of femininity.

In the body, Venus corresponds to several internal organs. The kidneys not only filter and purify the blood, they also maintain the stability of its composition. The parathyroid glands also perform a balancing and regulating function. The venous system, unlike the arteries, carries blood back to the heart. Venus is also associated with the female sex organs, particularly the ovaries.

Mars

Mars symbolizes self-preservation, survival, assertiveness, dominance, and territoriality. Crude, but to the point, it is the planet of war, combat, blood and sharp pointed objects. Soldiers, boxers, and firefighters will have an emphasized Mars. It is the planet of self-interest, competition and the striving for personal power. Mars, a traditionally masculine planet, is symbolic of the male as hunter and warrior.

Physiologically, Mars rules the muscles, which empower the body and allow it to move about. Control of one's muscles is needed in order to be autonomous and independent of others. In many ways, Mars could be associated with Freud's anal stage of development, with its emphasis on the self-control of toilet training. Mars also rules the arteries and the blood itself. Other parts of the body associated with Mars are the male sex glands, and the adrenal gland, which is activated when one's survival is threatened.

A Psychological Model for the Inner Planets

The psychological functions of the inner planets and the Moon can be understood as key points in a hypothetical model of the self.[11] In the drawing below the Sun represents the life force itself and stands at the center. Radiating from this center are four spokes, much like the four directions, that represent four developmental stages. The Moon stands at one point

---

11 See B. Scofield. *The Circuitry of the Self: Astrology and the Developmental Model.* One Reed Publications, 2000.

and represents the subconscious mind and the oral, bio-survival stage of development. Opposite to the Moon stands Mercury, representing the conscious mind and the language-using stage of human development. At opposite points on the other axis are Mars and Venus. Mars represents the muscle-control and power stage of development, Venus represents the social and sexual stage of development. Freud would recognize this as a model that contains his oral, anal, and genital stages of human development.

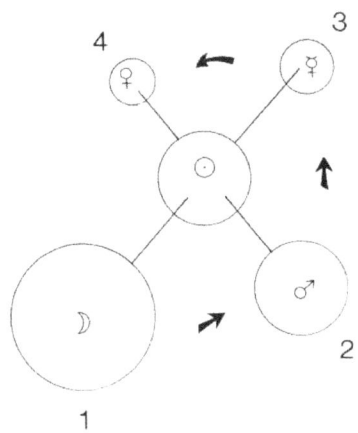

Figure 3. Hypothetical Model of the Self

This model suggests several things. First, and very much in line with the developmental models proposed by psychologists; it suggests that humans develop in stages and that these follow the order Moon, Mars, Mercury, Venus. The Moon stage, which is pre-verbal, extends from birth to about 2 years. During this time, our attachments, our feelings and our unconscious needs determine how we move forward in life. At about 2 years of age, just when Mars has completed one full cycle since birth, the Mars stage begins. During this period we learn to control our muscles, become more autonomous and learn to assert our power. The "terrible twos" set in during this Mars stage. At about 5 years of age the Mercury stage is dominant. We begin school at this time and learn to use words and language. Between ages 8 and 16 Venus is the dominant influence and we confront our sexuality and learn important social lessons.

Another implication of this model is that we take our key imprints for each stage during the time that it is active. For example, we learn how to get what we want for ourselves during the Mars period. If our experiences during this time were difficult, then our "Mars imprint" might become distorted and later cause problems that require attention. If the Moon, Mercury, Mars, or Venus are stressfully configured in a birth chart, it may suggest difficulties in each corresponding stage of childhood. It is possible to use astrology to provide valuable information to parents and educators concerning the development of children.

The Asteroids

Until about two hundred years ago, astrologers used just seven planets, those discussed so far plus Jupiter and Saturn. But since that time, two other large planets and many smaller bodies such as Pluto in the Kuiper Belt and numerous asteroids have been discovered (those that orbit the Sun in regular orbits and are of substantial size are also called dwarf or minor planets). In our solar system, the gap between Mars and Jupiter is filled with thousands of asteroids. Some astrologers place asteroids in birth charts and investigate their potential as symbols of very specific psychological functions.

Four asteroids, Ceres, Pallas, Juno, and Vesta, were discovered within a few years of each other at the beginning of the 19th century. These four appear to represent specific aspects of the female archetype represented by the Moon and Venus in general. Ceres, which is big enough to be classified as a dwarf planet, has to do with nurturing and agriculture. Pallas is intellectual and has to do with feminine crafts, weaving, and pattern perception. Juno is linked to women's arts, female decoration, and female power. Vesta has to do with dedication, celibacy, sacrifice, and service. Hygeia, the fourth largest asteroid, was discovered in 1849 and has been linked to health, wellness, purification and daily hygiene. Prominence of one or more of these asteroids in a birth chart suggests a concern with these issues.

Jupiter and Saturn

Beyond Mars are the two largest planets in the solar system, Jupiter and Saturn. These planets are many times larger than Mercury, Venus, and Mars combined. Jupiter is a massive body with gravitational power that pulls on comets and even regulates the positions of other planets and asteroids. In astrology, Jupiter and Saturn, in contrast to the inner planets, which are more personal and descriptive of the individual self, symbolize our experience and adaptation to the larger social reality around us. Together, Jupiter and Saturn are the planets signifying the larger human communities in which we live, their rules and their benefits.

Jupiter and Saturn take much longer to orbit the Sun than do the inner planets. The Moon spends 2.5 days in each sign of the zodiac, Mercury around three weeks, Venus about a month, and Mars about six weeks. In contrast, Jupiter spends about a year in each sign, and Saturn 2.5 years. In both size and motion, Jupiter and Saturn have a very different nature than the inner planets and this is reflected in their observed astrological effects. Astronomers classify Jupiter and Saturn, and also Uranus and Neptune, as gas giants because they are made up of mostly dense gases surrounding a small rocky and metallic core.

Jupiter

Jupiter is the planet of growth and is associated with acquisition, whether this be intellectual, material, or physical. People with an emphasized Jupiter are often intellectual seekers, information collectors, money-makers, or they may simply be physically large. Jupiter represents the urge to expand one's horizons via traveling or learning. It has to do with the larger view of things, views developed in the fields of philosophy, religion, and legal studies. Socially, Jupiter represents generous and benevolent people, judges, ministers, and speculators.

Jupiter is also traditionally the planet of optimism and positive thinking. It is associated with luck, which is essentially a matter of timing – being in the right place at the right time. Ancient astrologers considered Jupiter the most beneficial planet of all. However, too much of something can be as detrimental as too little. Jupiter is the planet that is active as an astrological force behind habitual excesses, over-production, and obesity. In the body, Jupiter is linked to the liver, the largest organ, the hips and thighs move us forward, and to the posterior lobe of the pituitary gland, which regulates growth.

Saturn

Saturn is the last of the visible planets known to the ancients and it marked the outer edge of the solar system. It is the planet of limits, boundaries, and barriers. It symbolizes laws, rules and regulations, and the need to establish and conform to realistic perspectives. Whereas Jupiter represents an outgoing energy, Saturn represents a force that contracts. In society, Saturn symbolizes hard workers, realists, farmers, distant authorities, law-makers, and government officials.

People with an emphasized Saturn are often serious, hard-working, goal-driven, and motivated by established and usually high standards. Status and reputation are important to the Saturn type. As the planet of responsibility, it can often weigh heavily on a person, leading to feelings of duty and obligation. Saturn represents the need to consolidate and make secure, in terms of both ideas and materials. Anatomically, Saturn rules the bones and teeth, which are the hard parts that give the body a definite structure, and the skin, which defines the visible outer limit of the body.

Chiron: A Transitional Object

In 1977, astronomer Charles Kowal discovered what appeared to be a minor planet orbiting between Saturn and Uranus. In one part of its elliptical orbit, this body gets closer to the Sun than Saturn; and in another part, it is farther from the Sun than Uranus ever gets. The orbit of this newly discovered object is representative of a link between the last known planet of the ancients with the first of the modern, outer planets, and this gives it a unique place in the astrological system of planetary symbols.

Astronomers soon named Kowal's new object Chiron, after the king of the centaurs. Although these creatures were part human, they were beasts below the waist, so the centaurs were noted for their savagery and lust. But Chiron was the exception: a teacher and a wounded healer. The consensus of many independent astrological investigators seems to be that Chiron symbolizes several issues including health, healing (chiropractic), disabilities, and also teaching and learning in general. Astrologers have also found that Chiron symbolizes the independent and solitary qualities of a maverick. In 1988, astronomical research determined that Chiron exhibits some of the characteristics of a comet. Chiron, part asteroid and part comet, is leading astronomers towards a better understanding of the smaller bodies in our solar system. Other bodies similar to Chiron have since been discovered and, as a group, are called centaurs.

The Outer Planets

The gas giants Uranus and Neptune, and the dwarf planet Pluto, were discovered by telescope. Except for Uranus, which can be seen only under ideal conditions by those with very sharp eyes, these planets are beyond the range of our normal human senses. Astrologically, they symbolize forces that are capable of changing both the individual and the community. They represent the disruptive forces that occur from time to time in a person's life, in the lives of a generation, or in the life of a community. They move so slowly that entire generations have Pluto or Neptune in the same sign at birth. The location of these planets in a person's birth chart indicates his or her capacity to change, or to be an agent of change. Astrologers have noted that historical events occurring at the time these planets were discovered seem to correlate with their astrological meaning.

Uranus

Uranus was the first of the outer planets to be discovered. It was unexpectedly sighted in 1781 by the astronomer William Herschel while he was exploring the heavens with a telescope in his backyard. This discovery took place as the American Revolution ended and the French Revolution began. Astrologers consider these disruptive events, which have transformed society and became examples for revolutions ever since, give insights into the astrological influences of Uranus. The year 1781 also marked the time when the Industrial Revolution became self-perpetuating, and it was also the year that a human left the ground for the first time in a hot-air balloon. Astrologers note that most of our modern political, technical, and industrial realities had their origins around the time that Uranus was discovered.

Astrologically, Uranus symbolizes discovery, technology, instability, and change. It often acts suddenly and unpredictably, disturbing the normal flow of events. It symbolizes advanced technology, invention, ingenuity, deviation, and experiment. Uranus is often described as a higher octave of Mercury because it appears to operate on an extremely mental level. Like Mercury, it is linked to the nervous system, but it is also considered the ruler of the pineal gland, which lies near the brain. Psychologically, Uranus represents the will, the focused intent of a person. People with an emphasized Uranus are often stubborn, rigid, and original characters who may not harmonize with others due to their strong sense of independence. Socially, Uranus represents individualists, radicals, reformers, rebels, inventors, and also people with an interest in socially transforming technology such as computers and electronics.

Neptune

Strange coincidences, misinformation, and chaos are some of Neptune's astrological properties. The circumstances of Neptune's discovery appear to have correlations with this planet's astrological effect. Neptune was sighted in 1846 by two astronomers working independent of each other under confusing and controversial circumstances. At the time of Neptune's discovery, the world saw many revolts and uprising, the intensification of the anti-slavery movement, the introduction of ether as an anesthetic, the development of photography (where chemicals produce images), the rise of Spiritualism, the beginnings of a decadent movement in the arts, and the publication of the seminal works on communism by Karl Marx.

Like Uranus, Neptune has something to do with visionaries and movements toward the future, but it operates on the level of the feelings and instincts. Uranus is super-mental and willful, but Neptune is super-sensitive and psychic. Neptune is the spiritual and artistic high, a state of mind where distinctions do not exist. Uranus makes for sharp distinctions: black and white, positive and negative. Neptune symbolizes no boundaries, is collectivist socially and represents a dissolving force, where everything blends into everything else often resulting in chaos. In some respects, receptive Neptune is like a higher octave of the Moon.

People with an emphasized Neptune are typically idealistic, artistic, poetic, dreamy, psychic, and imaginative. They usually base crucial life decisions entirely on their feelings and they often sacrifice their lives to another person, or to an ideal. Their philosophical or religious beliefs rule their lives and drive them to do what they can to bring the ideal into reality. With Neptune there is the drive to lose one's ego, to sacrifice for the greater good, to become selfless, or seek a unified state of consciousness. These people may be complex, but they are often ones who move humanity towards the future. Socially, Neptune symbolizes social service workers such as nurses, dancers, artists, visionaries, romantics, spiritualists, psychics, addicts of all sorts, and masters of deception.

Pluto

For many years Pluto marked the outermost limit of the known solar system. This small body, smaller than Earth's Moon, was discovered in 1930, the time of the stock market crash, the rise of Hitler, and the prominence of underworld of organized crime. The world was in crisis, but out of this crisis a global society emerged. A major force in creating the global society was television, a medium for the masses that was developed around the time of Pluto's discovery. When the programming of television became transferred to the internet, Pluto's potential in this medium was realized. Pluto is less of a personal planet and much more a planet of mass society and large populations in general.

Pluto is not at all like the gas giants. Astronomers classify it as a dwarf planet located in a region called the Kuiper Belt, although it does cut into the orbit of Neptune when its orbit brings it closest to the Sun. It is physically small, has an active surface and is orbited by five moons, one of which is half its size! In astrology, Pluto rules survival itself and the crises of death and regeneration. It symbolizes the power of evolution and inevitable transformations, beginnings and endings, birth and death. It rules sex and reproduction, the means by which life regenerates itself and "survives" beyond death. In Plutonian matters, the needs of the species outweigh the needs of the individual. Death makes room for birth and the community lives on.

People with an emphasized Pluto tend to take life very seriously and some will react to challenging events as if their very lives were at stake. Others find fulfillment in activities that change and transform the world around them, or they may be concerned with eliminating that which is no longer useful. In the body, Pluto is associated with the sex glands, eliminative organs, and possibly with the DNA found in cells.

Pluto is also associated with hidden things, secrets, and the dark. Like Mars, it symbolizes the power urge, but Pluto's power is more subtle. Whereas Mars rules hand-to-hand combat, Pluto rules psychological warfare, espionage, and nuclear power. A negative Pluto type can be obsessive, jealous, possessive, demanding, domineering, and over-whelming. Because it is the power and survival of the group that is at issue under Pluto, this planet works best for people who have learned to trust and share. Socially, Pluto is symbolic of people involved with power networking, the corporate world, taxation, insurance, and banking. It also has connections to medicine, particularly surgery, plumbing, archaeology and investigating in general.

Planets beyond Pluto

Pluto is technically part of the Kuiper Belt, a region of the solar system that contains many asteroids, comets and minor planets located beyond the orbit of Neptune. The orbital periods of these bodies range from a few hundred years to over one thousand. Bodies roughly the size of Pluto exist and some of these are being studied by astrologers. One is Eris which has an orbital period of about 560 years and seems to symbolize mischief and discord. Haumea, Makemake, Orchus and Quaoar are other minor planets in the Kuiper Belt, all named for mythical figures from different traditional cultures. Their astrological meanings are a work in progress, discoveries that result from the observations of many astrologers.

The primary planets and their astrological meanings

☉ Sun: The Center

Physical: The heart and the spine, the life of the body, physical strength and vitality, bodily integrity, the will to live.

Psychological: The need for attention, ego-strength, self-esteem, confidence, primary motivations, self-integration.

Social: The hero, the authority, the father, leaders, rulers, male energies in general.

☾ Moon: The Reactor

Physical: The mouth, the stomach, metabolism, digestion, the womb and breasts.

Psychological: Moods and feelings, the subconscious mind, the right brain, instinctive responses and habits, interests, protective urges, the need to nurture or be nurtured.

Social: Family, relations based on feelings, emotional attachments, parenting, mother figures, herd (or hive) consciousness, the general public, female energies in general.

☿ Mercury: The Thinker and Communicator

Physical: The nervous system, the left brain, the eyes, the hands, breathing, the lungs.

Psychological: mental activity, mind, rationalizations, relativism, coordination, adaptability, expression.

Social: Communications (speech, phones, writing, translation, etc.), mobility and transportation (cars, bikes, planes), agents, go-betweens.

♀ Venus: The Lover

Physical: The kidneys, veins, regulating hormones, female reproductive organs, gonads.

Psychological: Attractions, love, romance, courtship, mating, relationship skills, cooperation with others.

Social: Art, beauty, artistic taste, culture, evaluation, balance, peace, negotiations, agreements, marriage, consultants, counselors.

♂ Mars: The Warrior

Physical: The muscles, blood and arteries, immune system, male sex organs, acute health issues, cuts, bruises, burns.

Psychological: initiative, self-assertion, bravery, aggression, personal power, establishment of domain, self-preservation, impulse, rage, passion.

Social: Activity, construction, competition, sports, conflict, war.

♃ Jupiter: The Growth Provoker

Physical: The hips, thighs, sciatic nerve, liver, and posterior pituitary gland, conditions of enlarging and stretching.

Psychological: Confidence, positive attitude, optimism, humor, generosity, risk-taking, liberal, broad-minded, tolerant.

Social: Growth and increase, overpopulation, moral issues, exaggeration, volume, abundance, wealth.

♄ Saturn: The Limiter

Physical: Bones, teeth, the skeleton, knees, the skin, hearing, chronic health issues, conditions of contraction and narrowing.

Psychological: self-control, restraint, discipline, endurance, patience, persistence, organization, realism, resourcefulness, frugality.

Social: Rules and regulations, laws, contracts, structure and form, permanence, authority figures, restriction, separation, obstacles, delays.

♅ Uranus: The Deviator

Physical: Circulation system, the ankles, nervous system, and pineal gland, neuropathies.

Psychological: The will, individualism, eccentricity, independence, mental instability, tension, irregularities.

Social: Reforms, rebellions, revolution, anarchy, invention, originality, change, experimentation.

♆ Neptune: The Idealist

Physical: The feet, lymphatic system, thalamus, fluid issues.

Psychological: Visions, dreams, altered states of consciousness, emotions, hyper-sensitivity, anxiety, self-deception, confusion.

Social: Idealism, socialism, refinement, sensitivity, confusion, lack of distinctions, dreams, drugs, denial, untruths, myths, the spiritual.

♇ Pluto: The Transformer

Physical: The eliminative and reproductive organs, DNA, cell disfunction.

Psychological: Psychic disturbances, territorial reactions, power issues, sexual urges, compulsions, intensity, the need to change oneself.

Social: Change, crisis, renewal, purification, power, domination, manipulations, secrecy, conspiracy, elimination, death and rebirth, regeneration.

The Ephemeris

Astrologers use a table of planetary positions called an ephemeris to locate planets for any given day. An ephemeris lists the daily position in degrees and minutes of each planet at midnight or noon in Greenwich, England. In order to determine the position of a planet at a time other than midnight or noon Greenwich Mean Time (GMT or UT), astrologers perform simple mathematical interpolations. Below is a sample page of an ephemeris produced by Astrolabe Solar Fire software. If you look closely you will see that Saturn and Pluto were in conjunction (same degree) on the 12th of the month and Venus was square (90 degrees apart) to Mars on the 27th.

GMT +00:00 Tropical Geocentric Long	S.T. hh:mm:ss	Moon ☽	Sun ☉	Mercury ☿	Venus ♀	Mars ♂	Jupiter ♃	Saturn ♄	Uranus ♅	Neptune ♆	Pluto ♇
Jan 1 2020	06:40:29	16°♓08'	10°♑00'	04°♑23'	14°♒24'	28°♏23'	06°♑40'	21°♑23'	02°♉41' ℞	16°♓15'	22°♑23'
Jan 2 2020	06:44:25	28°♓01'	11°♑01'	05°♑57'	15°♒38'	29°♏03'	06°♑54'	21°♑30'	02°♉41'	16°♓17'	22°♑25'
Jan 3 2020	06:48:22	09°♈53'	12°♑02'	07°♑32'	16°♒51'	29°♏43'	07°♑07'	21°♑37'	02°♉40'	16°♓18'	22°♑27'
Jan 4 2020	06:52:18	21°♈50'	13°♑04'	09°♑07'	18°♒04'	00°♐24'	07°♑21'	21°♑44'	02°♉40'	16°♓19'	22°♑29'
Jan 5 2020	06:56:15	03°♉55'	14°♑05'	10°♑43'	19°♒18'	01°♐04'	07°♑35'	21°♑51'	02°♉39'	16°♓20'	22°♑31'
Jan 6 2020	07:00:11	16°♉14'	15°♑06'	12°♑19'	20°♒31'	01°♐45'	07°♑49'	21°♑58'	02°♉39'	16°♓22'	22°♑33'
Jan 7 2020	07:04:08	28°♉50'	16°♑07'	13°♑55'	21°♒44'	02°♐25'	08°♑03'	22°♑06'	02°♉39'	16°♓23'	22°♑35'
Jan 8 2020	07:08:05	11°♊46'	17°♑08'	15°♑32'	22°♒58'	03°♐05'	08°♑16'	22°♑13'	02°♉39'	16°♓24'	22°♑37'
Jan 9 2020	07:12:01	25°♊04'	18°♑09'	17°♑09'	24°♒11'	03°♐46'	08°♑30'	22°♑20'	02°♉39'	16°♓26'	22°♑39'
Jan 10 2020	07:15:58	08°♋44'	19°♑10'	18°♑47'	25°♒24'	04°♐26'	08°♑44'	22°♑27'	02°♉39'	16°♓27'	22°♑41'
Jan 11 2020	07:19:54	22°♋44'	20°♑12'	20°♑25'	26°♒37'	05°♐07'	08°♑58'	22°♑34'	02°♉38'	16°♓28'	22°♑43'
Jan 12 2020	07:23:51	07°♌00'	21°♑13'	22°♑03'	27°♒50'	05°♐48'	09°♑11'	22°♑41'	02°♉39' D	16°♓30'	22°♑45'
Jan 13 2020	07:27:47	21°♌27'	22°♑14'	23°♑42'	29°♒03'	06°♐28'	09°♑25'	22°♑48'	02°♉39'	16°♓31'	22°♑47'
Jan 14 2020	07:31:44	06°♍00'	23°♑15'	25°♑22'	00°♓16'	07°♐09'	09°♑39'	22°♑55'	02°♉39'	16°♓33'	22°♑49'
Jan 15 2020	07:35:40	20°♍31'	24°♑16'	27°♑02'	01°♓29'	07°♐49'	09°♑52'	23°♑02'	02°♉39'	16°♓34'	22°♑51'
Jan 16 2020	07:39:37	04°♎57'	25°♑17'	28°♑42'	02°♓41'	08°♐30'	10°♑06'	23°♑09'	02°♉39'	16°♓36'	22°♑53'
Jan 17 2020	07:43:34	19°♎14'	26°♑18'	00°♒23'	03°♓54'	09°♐11'	10°♑19'	23°♑17'	02°♉39'	16°♓38'	22°♑55'
Jan 18 2020	07:47:30	03°♏17'	27°♑19'	02°♒04'	05°♓06'	09°♐51'	10°♑33'	23°♑24'	02°♉40'	16°♓39'	22°♑57'
Jan 19 2020	07:51:27	17°♏08'	28°♑20'	03°♒45'	06°♓19'	10°♐32'	10°♑47'	23°♑31'	02°♉40'	16°♓41'	22°♑59'
Jan 20 2020	07:55:23	00°♐44'	29°♑22'	05°♒27'	07°♓31'	11°♐13'	11°♑00'	23°♑38'	02°♉41'	16°♓42'	23°♑01'
Jan 21 2020	07:59:20	14°♐07'	00°♒23'	07°♒10'	08°♓44'	11°♐54'	11°♑14'	23°♑45'	02°♉41'	16°♓44'	23°♑03'
Jan 22 2020	08:03:16	27°♐17'	01°♒24'	08°♒53'	09°♓56'	12°♐34'	11°♑27'	23°♑52'	02°♉42'	16°♓46'	23°♑05'
Jan 23 2020	08:07:13	10°♑14'	02°♒25'	10°♒36'	11°♓08'	13°♐15'	11°♑41'	23°♑59'	02°♉42'	16°♓48'	23°♑07'
Jan 24 2020	08:11:09	22°♑59'	03°♒26'	12°♒19'	12°♓21'	13°♐56'	11°♑54'	24°♑06'	02°♉43'	16°♓49'	23°♑09'
Jan 25 2020	08:15:06	05°♒33'	04°♒27'	14°♒03'	13°♓33'	14°♐37'	12°♑07'	24°♑13'	02°♉44'	16°♓51'	23°♑11'
Jan 26 2020	08:19:03	17°♒55'	05°♒28'	15°♒46'	14°♓45'	15°♐18'	12°♑21'	24°♑20'	02°♉44'	16°♓53'	23°♑13'
Jan 27 2020	08:22:59	00°♓08'	06°♒29'	17°♒29'	15°♓56'	15°♐59'	12°♑34'	24°♑27'	02°♉45'	16°♓55'	23°♑15'
Jan 28 2020	08:26:56	12°♓11'	07°♒30'	19°♒13'	17°♓08'	16°♐39'	12°♑47'	24°♑34'	02°♉46'	16°♓57'	23°♑17'
Jan 29 2020	08:30:52	24°♓08'	08°♒31'	20°♒55'	18°♓20'	17°♐20'	13°♑00'	24°♑41'	02°♉47'	16°♓59'	23°♑19'
Jan 30 2020	08:34:49	06°♈00'	09°♒32'	22°♒37'	19°♓32'	18°♐01'	13°♑13'	24°♑48'	02°♉48'	17°♓00'	23°♑21'
Jan 31 2020	08:38:45	17°♈51'	10°♒33'	24°♒18'	20°♓43'	18°♐42'	13°♑27'	24°♑55'	02°♉49'	17°♓02'	23°♑22'
Feb 1 2020	08:42:42	29°♈46'	11°♒34'	25°♒58'	21°♓55'	19°♐23'	13°♑40'	25°♑02'	02°♉50'	17°♓04'	23°♑24'

Other points used in astrology

☊☋ Lunar Nodes

Nodes are not physical objects, they simply mark the intersection of the plane defined by the Moon's (or a planet's) orbit with the orbital plane of the Earth. Since the intersection of two planes produces a straight line, there are two nodal points in the zodiac usually designated as north and south nodes. The Moon's nodes have long been in common use by astrologers. The lunar north node (symbol shown) and south node (same symbol but upside down) are generally interpreted as sensitive points in the birth chart that symbolize social networks and connections with family, friends, and other nurturing associations. The north node denotes new connections, the south node what has already been processed, this being reflected in older names for the lunar nodes, the north node as the dragon's head (intake), the south as the dragon's tail (outake). In Hindu astrology, the north node (Rahu) and the south node (Ketu) are so important that they are elevated to the status of planets.

The Part of Fortune

The Part of Fortune is one of a large number of "parts" or "lots" determined with geometry and planetary positions and often conditioned by whether a birth occurred during the day or night (called "sect" in ancient astrology). The Part of Fortune for a day birth is located by adding the phase angle between the Sun and Moon to the degree of the zodiacal sign rising at that time, i.e. the Ascendant.[12] Think of it this way: if the Moon was 90 degrees ahead of the Sun in the natal chart, put the Sun on the Ascendant and the Part of Fortune will be where the Moon would be, 90 degrees ahead. For a night birth, the Moon is placed on the Ascendant and the Sun's angle will then mark the Part of Fortune. Although it is a derived point in the zodiac, the Part of Fortune is held to be symbolic of opportunity and possible good

---

12 The formula for the Part of Fortune for a day birth is Ascendant + Moon − Sun, for a night birth is Ascendant + Sun − Moon.

fortune. There are many other parts derived from various planet combinations and determined by a similar formula.

Hypothetical Planets

During the 20th century, some astrologers have proposed the existence and astrological use of planets that have not been verified astronomically. The orbits and symbolic nature of many of these hypothetical planets have been determined on the basis of astrological observation alone. Most of them have orbits that would place them in the range of the Kuiper Belt. While most astrologers do not use them in their work, the Hamburg School of Astrology in Germany, also known as Uranian Astrology in the U.S., utilizes eight of these hypothetical planets in their methodology. Transpluto, also known as Persephone, is one hypothetical planet whose orbital parameters have been calculated by astronomers but which has not yet been sighted. It is believed by some astrologers to symbolize female maturity, ecological balance, and the dynamics of gender-balanced relationships. Other non-physical points are used by some astrologers. One of these is called the Dark Moon Lilith, a point (apogee/2nd foci) derived from the slightly elliptical orbit of the Moon.

The Fixed Stars

Some astrologers use stars for an expanded interpretation of the astrological chart. These stars are called "fixed" because they don't have an orbital motion like the planets and remain more or less in the same place with respect to the other stars around them. Certain stars such as the "royal stars" (Aldebaran, Regulus, Antares, and Fomalhaut) have been used by astrologers since ancient times. Their degree positions in the zodiac seem to have a definite "charge" to them, and planets located near them appear to gain in power.

The fixed stars do not move relative to each other (except for minor adjustments over thousands of years), but they do exhibit measurable movement relative to the equinoxes and solstices. This motion is called the precession of the equinoxes, whereby the stars shift against the equinoxes at the rate of about one degree of the zodiac every 72 years. A number of dramatic astrological predictions, based on this slow movement, have involved the movement of a point in an astrological chart to one fixed star or another.

5

Aspects and Alignments

Of the four primary sets of symbols in astrology, planets are clearly the most important. Their positions in the sky and in the astrological chart are measured along the zodiac in degrees, 30 degrees per each sign. The specific angular separations between the planets, called aspects, take planetary symbolism one step further in that they show two things. First, aspects show the blending between two or more planets, which produces a more complex pallette of astrological effects. Aspects also reveal the phase that any two planets are in, that is where in their cycles they happen to be at the moment. If the astrological chart were an electronic circuit board, the planets would be the transistors and chips, and the aspects would be the wires or metallic tracks that link them and reveal their relationships with each other.

An aspect is a specific kind of alignment that occurs when two planets are separated by a key geometric angle. The aspects are measured along the zodiac, which is the ecliptic or Sun's path. For example, planets on the ecliptic that are separated by about 90 degrees (one quarter of the 360-degree circle) are in a square aspect. Those separated by 120 degrees, or a third of a circle, are in a trine aspect, and so forth. While about ten aspects are commonly used by modern astrologers, only two planetary relationships were recognized in ancient Mesopotamia, where astrology originated. These were the conjunction (an angular separation of zero degrees) and the opposition (an angular separation of 180 degrees). Three others, the sextile, square, and trine, were added by the Greeks, who applied their knowledge of geometry to the astrology of the Near East. These five aspects as a group are called the Ptolemaic aspects. Much later, Johannes Kepler, the great astronomer-astrologer, added several minor aspects to the list. In the diagram below, the Ptolemaic aspects, extending from a point located in the middle of Aries (-15 degrees), are shown.

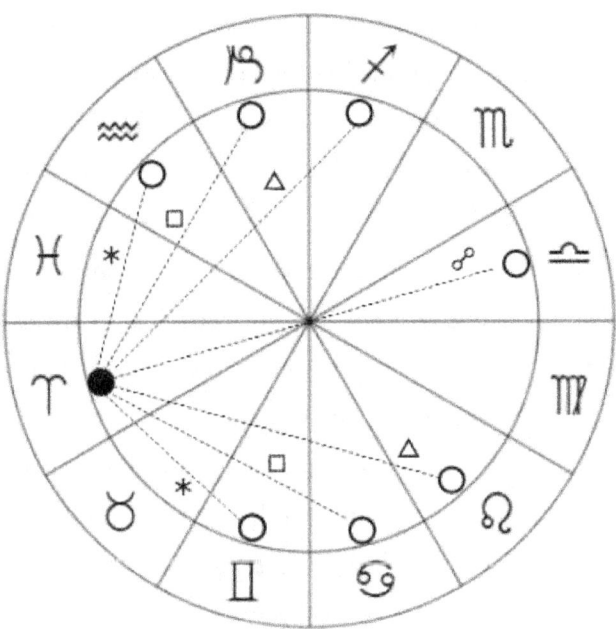

Figure 4. The Ptolemaic Aspects.

Aspects blend planetary principles. For example, the Sun alone symbolizes confidence, integrity and self-worth. If the Sun is square or opposition to Saturn, however, these qualities will be blunted. A person born with Sun square or opposition to Saturn will have to work harder to achieve self-worth, but that may make them stronger. A person with the Sun square or opposition to Jupiter may be over-confident and bring about problems in that way. The Moon conjunct Venus can be very emotional but the Moon conjunct Mars can be impulsive. There are many combinations of aspects and entire books have been written that delineate each combination of planets and aspects.

Students of numerology will notice that each of the aspects are based on the division of the circle by a number. In fact, this is one area in which numerology and astrology overlap. It was the Greek astrologers, probably influenced by the scientist and numerologist Pythagoras, who were behind the development of the aspects. A comparison of the nature of the aspects with traditional numerology will reveal deep similarities.

It is helpful to think of the aspects in terms of vibrations and harmonics. The division of the circle of the zodiac by each number, called the fundamental, produces a specific tone or harmonic. The same is true of music. On stringed instruments an open string produces a fundamental tone. If you divide the length of the string into half, or thirds or fourths, you will find these points to be harmonics that will produce a clear tone without having to press the string down onto the neck (fretted or unfretted) of the instrument. Johannes Kepler understood this connection between the physics of music and astrology, and also between the orbits of the planets, and all three were part of his theory of everything.

The Principal Aspects: Harmonics 1 through 12

Conjunctions ☌

The conjunction is the most powerful planetary alignment. It occurs when two planets occupy the same, or nearly the same, degree of the zodiac and marks the beginning of the cycle between them. It represents a division of the 360 degrees of the circle by one. The circle represents completeness, a condition in which all things are the same – merged and unified. The conjunction of two planets likewise symbolizes a fusion of their principles. For example, Saturn conjunct the Sun suggests that the cold of Saturn is conjoined with the heat of the Sun. Saturn is warmed up, but the Sun is cooled down. The new Moon is actually a conjunction of the Sun and Moon.

Aspects and Alignments

Oppositions ☍

Division of the circle by two produces the opposition, where the planets are separated by 180 degrees. This aspect marks the halfway point in a cycle. With the opposition, the qualities of the planets are not blended as in the conjunction; they are separated yet forced to co-exist. The opposition has mixed qualities and some combinations of planets fare better when in this aspect than others. The full Moon is the opposition between Sun and Moon.

Trines △

Division of the circle by three produces the trine, or 120 degrees. Two planets in trine work well together; they are in phase or in balance with each other. Symbolically, the number one is manifestation, two is challenge, and three is harmony. In other words, one is the thesis, two is the antithesis, and three is the synthesis: the resolution of the dialectic, the bridging of the gap. The trine is stable, like a triangle. The triangle is such a solid form that bridge-builders often utilize its shape. There are two trines in any cycle, one at 120 degrees, the other 240 degrees from it. Three planets spaced equidistant from each other, 120 degrees apart, create what is known as a Grand Trine. This powerful configuration is generally stable and strong, but such extreme stability is not always a good thing because it can indicate resistant to change.

Squares □

Division of the circle by four produces the square, or 90 degrees. The square is tense and stressful, yet its demands often result in action and productivity. Although two planets in square are out of phase with each other, this aspect forces the two to work together toward practical ends. In this respect the square is not such a negative aspect. There are two squares in a cycle of two planets, one at 90 degrees, the other at 270 degrees. The quarters of the Moon occur when the Sun and Moon are in square. Four planets in square to each other produce what is called a Grand Cross. This is a particularly tense configuration requiring a constant effort to maintain a balance between the four points. Many people with such a configuration in their charts become stressed, while others manage the aspect well and become extremely productive and successful. Another challenging configuration is the T-square where one planet is square to two others that are in opposition.

Quintiles and Biquintiles Q Bq

Dividing the circle by five produces the quintile, or 72 degrees. Because 72 degrees is harder to spot than multiples of 30 degrees, this aspect is frequently overlooked and therefore not used by many astrologers. Overall, it is a positive aspect that promotes creativity and productivity in a natural way. The biquintile is 144 degrees, or twice the quintile, and has a similar effect.

Sextiles ✶

Division of the circle by six produces the sextile, or 60 degrees. Like the quintile, this aspect is considered positive in that it allows the planets to function together harmoniously. However, it works in less creative and natural ways than does the quintile and is not so natural and easy to work with as the trine. The sextile symbolizes opportunities or possibilities that need work or attention in order to be realized or reach completion.

Septiles S

Dividing the circle by seven produces the septile, an aspect that is close to 51 degrees plus about 25 minutes (51° 25'). Seven is the first number that does not divide exactly into 360. Numbers that have this property are sometimes called irrational. This strange aspect, rarely used by astrologers in the past because it was hard to calculate (but now handled easily with computers), is found in the charts of those who reach for the unattainable. For example, it is frequently found in the charts of those devoted to religion and spirituality. Multiples of 51° 25', in addition to the septile, are the biseptile (102° 58') and the triseptile (154° 17').

Aspects and Alignments

Semisquares and Sesquiquadrates ∠ ⚏

Dividing the circle by eight produces the semisquare (or octile), which is 45 degrees. The semisquare is half of a square. Like the square, it symbolizes difficulties and it tends to operate practically, directly, and immediately. It is regarded by astrologers as moderately stressful, but potentially productive. The sesquiquadrate (a.k.a. sesquisquare or tri-octile) is 135 degrees, or three times the semisquare. It is very similar to the semisquare.

Noviles, Deciles, and Elevenths

Division of the circle by nine, ten, and eleven produces aspects that are only rarely used by astrologers. The novile and decile are said to be moderately favorable while the eleventh, the second lowest irrational number, is said to be difficult. The labeling of aspects as favorable and difficult (or challenging) is really the product of hard-working astrologers who are pressed by their clients to make black or white judgment calls. The real effects of these subtle aspects are difficult to convey to people not interested in nuance or deep self-knowledge. The truth is that no aspect is actually good or bad. Aspects are just what they are and we must do our best in working with them.

The Semisextile and Quincunx ⚺ ⚻

Division of the circle by twelve produces the semisextile, an aspect of 30 degrees. Since it links adjacent signs of the zodiac, which have very little in common, the effects of this aspect can vary. Most practicing astrologers consider it moderately inharmonious. The quincunx or inconjunct is 150 degrees (five times the semisextile). Its effects have been described as tradeoffs where the positives are balanced by the negatives, something that most people find dissatisfying.

Parallels and Contraparallels ∥ ⧣

There are two other planetary connections that are not measured along the ecliptic and are not based on division of the circle. The parallel occurs when two planets are equidistant from the celestial equator, and both are either north or south of it. An analogy using the terrestrial equator would liken both planets sharing the same geographical latitude. The contra-parallel occurs when two planets are equidistant from the celestial equator, but one is north and one is south. This is a symmetrical relationship relative to an axis or baseline. The parallel tends to work like a conjunction; the contraparallel like an opposition.

Hard vs. Soft Aspects

The opposition, square, semisquare, and sesquiquadrate are all aspects that show a potential for stress, crisis, response, and productivity. These aspects, often called hard or challenging aspects, are found in the charts of those who work hard or struggle for achievement. Great men and women seem to be driven by these powerful aspects which signify the need to balance conflicting planetary energies. Notice that these aspects are produced by the division of 360 by 2, 4 and 8. Trines and sextiles are often called soft or harmonious aspects and are considered to be somewhat lucky, indicators of benefits that come without working too hard. People with too many soft aspects are often not so strongly motivated to resolve challenges and inner tensions, and consequently they tend to be less visibly productive. These aspects are produced by the division of 360 by 3 and 6.

Major vs. Minor Aspects

In practice, most astrologers use the conjunction, opposition, trine, square, and sextile as major aspects. These aspects are traditionally known as the Ptolemaic aspects, named after the great scientist Claudius Ptolemy who lived in Egypt during the time of the Roman Empire and who wrote on astrology, among many other subjects. Minor aspects include the semisquare and sesquiquadrate, the quintile, the septile, and the semisextile and quincunx. There are also other, even smaller, minor aspects that are used by some astrologers. These include the 16th harmonic, sometimes called the semi-semisquare (22° 30'), and the 32nd harmonic (11° 15'). These aspects function only when they are exact or very close to exact.

The division of the circle by successively larger numbers creates an infinite number of harmonics or aspects, and each aspect thus created should theoretically have some effect. As the numbers get larger and the aspects become smaller, however, the effect becomes too subtle and the work involved requires complex techniques or it becomes meaningless. Kepler felt that some people respond to minor aspects (or higher harmonics) to a greater degree than others, he saw this as a matter of being sensitive to them.

Applying, Separating, and Orbs

In the preceding discussion, the aspects were considered as exact angular separations between planets. In practice, an exact aspect is very rare. More commonly, two planets in a chart may be separated by a figure that is close to, but does not equal, the exact angle. For example, two planets spaced 125 degrees apart are close to the distance of the trine which is 120 degrees. When the relative motions of the two planets involved in an aspect are considered in this regard, we can tell if the aspect was exact before a birth (or other event) or afterward. Applying aspects are those that were not yet complete at birth, separating aspects have already formed. For example, if the Moon and Mars were trine each other at birth, but the actual degree of the Moon in its sign was lower than that of Mars, the aspect is applying. Applying aspects have a charge or urgency to them, separating aspects not so much.

Astrologers regard each aspect as having a range of effect which is called its orb of influence. In general, the orbs for the conjunction and opposition are larger than those for the other aspects. Also the orbs for any aspect involving the Sun or Moon are generally larger than those for the other planets. Although there is no universally agreed upon set of orbs for the aspects, suggested values are given for each aspect in the summary below.

Aspects and Cycles

There are two types of planetary cycles. Sidereal cycles track the movement of a planet, or the Sun or Moon, relative to a star. This cycle is the time taken for the planet to orbit the Sun once. It is also called the planet's period and these are listed in the table near the beginning of Chapter 4. The second type of cycle is a synodic cycle which measures the time taken between successive conjunctions of two planets. The classic example is the synodic cycle of the Moon and Sun which we know as New Moon, first quarter, Full Moon and third quarter. In a synodic cycle, whether it be the Sun and Moon, the Sun and Venus, Mars and Saturn, or any other pair of planets, it is the aspects that mark the phases. When two planets are in opposition, they are midway through their synodic cycle. An understanding of aspects then involves an understanding of phase.

A Summary of the Aspects

Major Aspects

Below are the five traditional (Ptolemaic) astrological aspects in order of strength. Also included are four additional aspects used by most astrologers.

♂ **Conjunction**: 0 degrees or 360 degrees apart. This aspect represents the beginning and end of a cycle and the fusing of the principles of the planets involved in an unconscious way. Its net astrological effect depends on the nature of the planets. Orb: +/- 10 degrees.

☍ **Opposition**: 180 degrees. This aspect marks the midpoint of a cycle. It usually represents a division or a critical turning point. It can mean success as a result of awareness, objectivity, and perspective, or it can imply conflict and separation. It symbolizes the need for understanding. Orb: +/- 10 degrees.

△ **Trine**: 120 degrees. Said to be the most favorable aspect, the trine represents a state of balance and harmony between the planets involved and what they symbolize. Orb: +/- 7 degrees.

□ **Square**: 90 degrees. This may be the most stressful aspect because it usually demands action or change. It represents the struggle between incompatible elements, and the consequent need for adjustments. Orb: +/- 7 degrees.

✶ **Sextile**: 60 degrees. The sextile, being one-half the value of the trine, has traditionally been regarded as an aspect that presents opportunities that require some effort to realize. It represents a point of stability in a cycle, and is favorable, but not as strong, as the trine. Orb: +/- 4 degrees.

Minor Aspects

∠ **Semisquare**: 45 degrees. This aspect, being one-half the value of the square, represents a point of friction and agitation that demands a practical response. Orb: +/-3 degrees.

⬛ **Sesquisquare**: 135 degrees. This aspect is three times a semisquare and as such is similar in effect. Orb: +/- 3 degrees.

⋎ **Semisextile**: 30 degrees. This aspect represents the onset of awareness and the blending of different elements. It symbolizes a mild discomfort or instability. Orb: +/- 2 degrees.

⚻ **Quincunx**: 150 degrees. Similar to the semisextile, though possibly stronger and more noticeable. The quincunx symbolizes the awareness of incompatibility, which leads to tradeoffs and compromises. It is also associated with health issues. Orb: +/- 2 degrees.

Midpoints

Planetary positions in a birth chart can be seen as energy vectors pointing outwards from the center in specific directions. When two planets in aspect, their energies mix – with a range of possible results. Aspects, then, are a way of interpreting the blending of planetary influences. Another way is to locate the midpoint between any two planets.

To locate a midpoint between two planets take the sum of two planetary positions and divide by two. Here's an example:

> The Sun is at 10 degrees of Aries and the Moon is at 10 degrees of Taurus, the next sign. There are 30 degrees in a sign, so we have 10 for the Sun and 40 (30 + 10) for the Moon. Then we take the sum, which is 50, and divide by 2. The Sun/Moon midpoint is at 25 degrees of Aries. Calculating midpoints is facilitated by using what's called absolute longitude, the positioning of planets in degrees running from 0 to 359.

The midpoint of any two planets is a sensitive point in a chart where the qualities of the two planets come together in a unique blend. Using the above example, the Sun/Moon midpoint symbolizes the merging of the masculine and feminine principles in the chart. This is a point that says much about a person's relationships with the opposite sex. Very subtle astrological delineations can be made using midpoints, and even aspects to midpoints.

The German Hamburg School of Astrology, known in the United States as Uranian Astrology or Symmetrical Astrology, utilizes the concept of midpoints extensively. Planetary pictures are symmetrical alignments of planets that are not necessarily in aspect with each other. Groupings of planets that share a common midpoint, or axis, are considered to be very important.

6

Signs of the Zodiac

The zodiac is a division of the ecliptic, the Sun's path through the sky, into twelve equal sections. (The term ecliptic refers to the fact that eclipses can only occur when the Moon is precisely on the Sun's path.) The ecliptic is also the path of the Moon and the planets as they move through their orbits. This is because the shape of the solar system is basically a flattened disk. The division of the ecliptic into sections associated with constellations occurred in ancient Mesopotamia over 4 millennia ago. The exact sequence of events that led to the 12-sign zodiac is not fully understood, but by about 400 BCE the zodiac in use today had been established.

Why Twelve Signs?

In early times, humankind looked to the skies for a sense of order. One of the first applications of ancient sky-watching was the construction of calendars. The first calendars were based on the Moon's cycle, but lunar calendars are impractical for agricultural pursuits that depend on the timing of the seasons. A solar calendar, like that used by the Egyptians, is based on the seasons and is very regular, in contrast to the lunar calendars used by nomadic peoples that require periodic adjustments. Blending a lunar and solar calendar presents problems because the cycles of the Sun and Moon do not mesh perfectly. Astronomically, a year has 365.2422 days, and there are an average of 12.4 Full Moons per year. This means that, depending on when the first full Moon occurred, there could be either twelve or thirteen full Moons in any given year. In the search for linkages between lunar and solar cycles, early Near Eastern calendar makers probably sought round numbers, not fractions, and they ultimately settled on twelve. This division of the year by 12 was also reflected in the designation of 12 constellations that the Sun traveled through during the course of a year.

The twelve primary divisions of the zodiac are astronomical frames of reference that were created by cultures of the northern hemisphere. They are 30-degree spatial sections of the sky, not tangible objects like planets. Our twelve-sign zodiac has a central place in the Western astrological tradition, and nearly every practicing astrologer agrees that the signs do seem to work – they modify the characteristics of the planets that pass through them. This may be due to the fact that the tropical zodiac we use today marks stages in the seasonal cycle, the cycle around which living things have adapted, though this would pertain only to the movement of the Sun and would only be accurate in the northern hemisphere. Scientific tests of the zodiac have been attempted but results have been mixed, in part due to the difficulty of attaching units to personality traits and also poor study design.

The Zodiac and the Seasons

There are two types of zodiac: sidereal zodiacs, which are tied to the constellations, and the tropical, or seasonal, zodiac, which has retained the names of the constellations, but is actually defined by the equinoxes. It is the tropical zodiac that is most commonly used in Western astrology today. It starts with the vernal (spring) equinox, the place where the Sun is located on, or within a day of, March 20th every year. On this day, the day that the Sun enters the sign Aries, the Sun rises due east and sets due west. It also rises and sets on the east/west line on the day of the autumnal equinox, which is the first day that the Sun enters the sign Libra. The term equinox refers to the fact that, because the Sun rises due east and sets due west, the days and nights are of equal length (equinox means "equal night").

As the days progress following the vernal equinox, the Sun rises further and further north of due east and the days increase in length. At the summer solstice, the longest day of the year, the Sun rises at its northernmost rising position. But before beginning its six-month journey further and further south along the horizon, it appears for several days to rise at this same point. Thus the term solstice which means "Sun-stand-still."

The summer solstice marks the beginning of the sign Cancer. At the winter solstice, the shortest day of the year, the Sun rises at its southernmost point and marks the beginning of the sign Capricorn. These positions, which are known in astrology as the cusps or beginnings of the Cardinal signs, create the four quarters of the year, otherwise known as the seasons. This is the basis of all solar calendars. They track both the rising and setting positions of the Sun and measure the ratio of daylight to night, what biologists call photoperiod. Dividing each quarter of the year into three equal parts produces the twelve signs of the zodiac. It is then the Sun in its yearly cycle that establishes the zodiac.

The Quadruplicities or Qualities

Aries, Cancer, Libra, and Capricorn are called the cardinal signs because the Sun enters them at the beginning of each season. After each cardinal sign comes a fixed sign, and after each fixed sign comes a mutable sign. Then the whole cycle begins again with a cardinal sign. This grouping of signs is called the Quadruplicities. Other names for it are the Crosses, Qualities, or Modes.

People born with the Sun in cardinal signs (Aries, Cancer, Libra, Capricorn) tend to be quick, initiating, busy, natural starters who are often at their best when getting projects off the ground. They are sometimes too restless for work that involves a regular routine. Fixed signs, (Taurus, Leo, Scorpio, Aquarius) are usually solid, resistant to change, and strive for regularity. They can be enduring, consistent, and also stubborn. Mutable signs (Gemini,

Virgo, Sagittarius, Pisces) are often changeable, adaptable, and often involved in multiple projects. They tend to be flexible and may seem inconsistent because they can see both sides of an issue.

The Triplicities or Elements

Signs are also classified by element. The Fire signs (Aries, Leo, Sagittarius) tend to be spirited, active, and inspired. Earth signs (Taurus, Virgo, Capricorn) are typically practical, conservative, and concerned with the material world. The Air signs (Gemini, Libra, Aquarius) are usually mental, communicative, and social. Water signs (Cancer, Scorpio, Pisces) are sensitive, emotional, and intuitive.

The Polarities

Finally, the signs are grouped into two categories called the Polarities. Like a pulse, the sequence of signs in the zodiac alternates between signs of outgoing or masculine energies (Fire and Air) and signs of inward-turning or feminine energies (Earth and Water). Since the zodiacal signs are arranged in the sequence Fire, Earth, Air, Water, etc., they also alternate masculine, feminine, masculine, feminine, etc. (or +, -, +, -). Other words used to describe these two modifiers of the signs are as follows:

Fire and Air: yang, outward, masculine, positive, active, hot, light.
Earth and Water: yin, inward, feminine, negative, yielding, cold, dark.

The diagram below arranges the Qualities, Elements and Polarities around the cycle of the year which is anchored on the equinoxes and solstices. Many cultural holidays are located in time near the equinoxes and the solstices and some are located midway between them, the cross-quarter days.

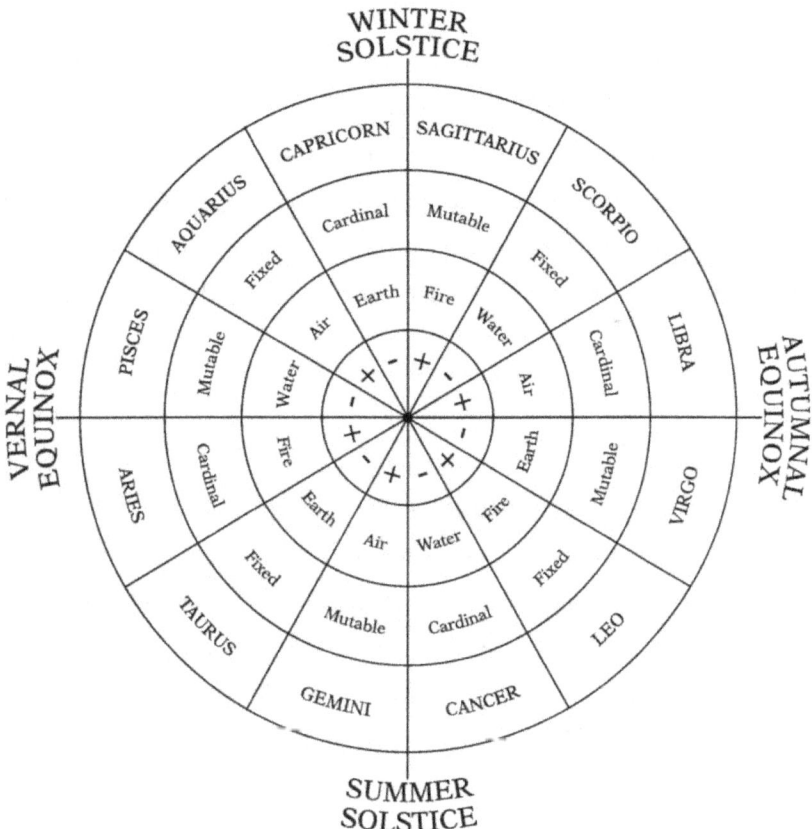

Figure 5. Cycle of the Year

The Signs through the Year

Aries, the first sign, begins when the Sun is at the vernal equinox; it symbolizes spring, the seed breaking its shell, the release of stored energy, and the birth of the self. Taurus has to do with substance, materials, possessions, and resources: what there is to work with. Gemini is concerned with information, communication, reaching out and manipulating the environment. Cancer has to do with nurturing, protection, domesticity, home and family; Leo with creativity, drama, the power and glory of the individual; Virgo with criticism, analysis, perfection, and discrimination.

What Astrology is ...And How to Use it

When applied to human life, the first six signs of the zodiac (from the spring to the fall equinox) symbolize the development or evolution of the individual. Aries is self-survival; Taurus is the use of resources and territory; and Gemini gets to know the environment by exploration, learning, and communicating. Cancer establishes the home and family, a base of operations, and a place for centering and protection; Leo masters life and dominates the world – and then Virgo becomes aware of flaws and of the need for adjustment and perfection.

While the first six signs are about the self, the second six are about the self in society. Each sign in the second half of the zodiac can be viewed as a more social manifestation of the opposite sign in the first half. Whereas Aries was the sign of self-encounter, Libra, its opposite, symbolizes basic relationship and cooperation – the encounter with another. Scorpio has to do with substance and materials, but specifically those that pertain to relationship, including sex, physical sharing, borrowing and lending. Sagittarius seeks a deeper, wider kind of knowledge than Gemini, traveling to more distant places, learning foreign languages, and coming to an understanding of cultural differences.

Capricorn has to do with finding one's place within the community. Whereas Cancer sought an emotionally secure center in the family, Capricorn seeks security in society through social position, status, and reputation. Aquarius symbolizes friendships and complex social experiments, the cooperation of individuals within groups. Whereas Leo led as an individual, Aquarius is more democratic and prefers to meet power needs through a group. Pisces has to do with the breakdown of social patterns. Whereas Virgo was critical of the self, Pisces is critical of society. It is the sign of the hermit, the monk, the artist, and the psychic, a symbol of the search for a higher social purpose. Both Aquarius and Pisces are signs of change, as if a breakdown were needed before the cycle could begin again at Aries.

Descriptions of the Signs

Below are the principal characteristics of each sign with a brief description of how each sign affects the Sun. Following this are brief delineations for the Moon and Ascendant, and the glyph (symbol) of the sign. You will find the Ascendant explained more fully in Chapter 8. Additional information includes the ruling planet, some keywords, body correspondences, and typical professions for each of the signs.

Aries is a Fire sign and the first sign of the zodiac. Those born with the Sun here are generally risk-tolerant and make choices in life that may be daring or pioneering, at least in comparison with their peers. They lead by going first, are generally active, direct, courageous, forceful, and quite impulsive people motivated strongly by self-interest. They meet the world in an immediate way, dislike complications and generally take a minimalist approach to things. Others often perceive this as being forceful, even headstrong. Aries types like their independence and often prefer to work alone as relationships can get in the way of their natural free-expression. Many are drawn to wild, untamed places and activities. They can be very constructive when their energies are harnessed, but the same energy can also fuel competitive instincts.

Life Issue: Who am I and what do I need?

Moon in Aries gives quick reactions and a need for action and excitement. Interest in sports and risk-taking is common with the Moon in this placement. Weaknesses include problems with self-control and a tendency to lose interest in things before bringing matters to a conclusion.

Ascendant in Aries gives a personality that takes the initiative in social matters. Self-interest is strong with this sign and there is a vital need for personal gratification. Those with Aries rising like their personal privacy, and they are often loners or soloists in important areas of their life. They also tend to be good problem solvers and they work quickly and efficiently.

Symbol: ♈

Ruling Planet: Mars

Body: Head, blood, muscles

Professions: Engineering, architecture, athletics, competition, self-employment, mechanical repair work, the military, construction.

Keywords: Impact. Direct. To the point. Basic. Simplicity. Primitive. Spartan. Bold. Risk. Lively. Forceful. Pioneering. Soloist.

Taurus is an Earth sign that is security-motivated and slow to change. Sun in Taurus is likely to be reliable, territorial, possessive, practical, determined, artistic, beauty-conscious, pleasure-loving, and self-indulgent. There is usually a strong conservative tendency in this sign, at least in terms of self-definition. Taurus likes permanence, consistency and comfort and finds money, valuable objects, and land and property to be of great interest. The Sun in Taurus often occurs in the charts of those who build things or develop systems and stay with them for long periods.

Life Issue: How do I manage my desire for security and comfort?

Moon in Taurus is mostly comfort-driven. People with this Moon sign generally have steady emotions, but they also have strong cravings for pleasures. Habits may be hard to break. Taste in most matters is generally mainstream and conservative. This is a materialistic signature in the chart – security is found in things of substance.

Ascendant in Taurus confers a strong sense of physicality and interest in appearance and beauty. Such people are often artistic and will often work to raise the aesthetic levels around them through design or decorating. This type of personality is quick to establish a standard social routine, but often gets stuck, finding it difficult to adjust or make changes.

Symbol: ♉

Ruling Planet: Venus

Body: Neck and throat, thyroid

Professions: business, investing, cashiering, banking, fashion and beauty, agriculture, landscaping, land ownership, art, music, design.

Keywords: Solidity. Down to earth. Enduring. Persistent, Reliable. Practical. Risk-adverse. Hard-headed. Natural. Luxury. Sensuous.

Gemini is an Air sign and likes to be constantly on the move absorbing information. Sun in Gemini types are quick, changeable, clever, curious, adaptable, intellectual, relativistic, and communicative. The sign is basically concerned with communication (talk, words, ideas, messages) and transportation (movement, mobility, linkage, connection). Varied experiences and interests lead to an understanding of the relationships between things. The Sun in Gemini is often a jack-of-all-trades and not known for great depth into any one subject.

Life Issue: What do I have to say, and how many can I have?

Moon in Gemini gives an interest in speaking, writing and teaching. People with the Moon in this sign are often busy with many projects and fully engaged in communicative activities, so they are sometimes stretched thin as a result. They tend to rationalize their emotions and prefer relationships that are strong on conversation and activities.

Ascendant in Gemini people have a lot of nervous energy and are often talkative and sometimes very witty. Their identities seem to be bound up with the themes of communication (phones, computers, books, paperwork) or transportation (cars, bicycles, walking, skating, etc.). Frequent changes are far more appealing to them than a regular routine.

Symbol: ♊

Ruling Planet: Mercury

Body: Nervous system, eyes, left brain, hands, lungs

Professions: Writing, speaking, communications, computers, teaching, driving, printing, secretarial work, translating.

Keywords: Flexibility. Light. Mobile. Varied. Adaptable. Neutral. Communicative. Message-oriented. Clever. Slippery. Hard to pin down.

Cancer, a Water sign, is motivated by what they sense to be important, basically feelings rather than rational, considerations. Life is driven by the need for a home base, domestic security – whatever gives the feeling of being at home. Typically, Cancerians are protective, resourceful, conservative, shrewd, touchy, romantic, imaginative, maternal, and domestic. They are fascinated by the past, both personal and historical, and are often collectors, preservationists and restorers. Cancer is the sign of the mother, and also of nourishment and eating. It is a very sensitive sign, not very comfortable with criticism, though it is drawn to public positions and leads by instinct.

Life Issue: What does home feel like?

Moon in Cancer indicates a personable nature with strong maternal or protective instincts. People with the Moon in this sign often become involved with the care of others, both in personal matters and professionally. Their concern and nurturing instincts may translate into success in what they do. There is often a love of nature and an attraction to water and desire to live near it.

Ascendant in Cancer types are very sensitive to the external world and can have higher than usual responses to other people. Some even have highly sensitive skin. This may cause them to develop a defensive persona. They interact emotionally with the world around them and are protective and parental toward others and their community. Their identity is typically built around care, concern, and preservation.

Symbol: ♋

Ruling Planet: Moon

Body: Mouth, stomach, breasts, womb

Professions: Public relations, banking, cooking, gardening, restaurant and hotel work, food industry, real estate, homemaking, home-based business, supporter of a tradition, historian, preservationist.

Keywords: Security. Homey. Traditional. Historical. Mother Nature. Collectible. Antique. Silver. The Sea. The Country.

Leo is a Fire sign and one of the more prominent and dominating signs of the zodiac. People with the Sun in Leo are usually creative, talented, dramatic, proud, authoritative, fond of entertainment or entertaining, lavish, forgiving, and generous. Leo is a sign with self-esteem and self-worth issues though they typically display great confidence when they present themselves to the world. Leo produces romantic lovers, artists, and also parents (who live out their self-worth issues through their children). Those with Sun in Leo are usually physically strong and make good teachers and role models. They lead by drawing people around them where they hold the center.

Life Issue: How important am I?

Moon in Leo gives a strong interest in performing of one kind or another, including teaching. The need for attention from others, along with the need to develop their talents, is very great and most people with this Moon sign will be found in creative fields or having (and working with) children. They can be strong and devoted parents. Stubbornness is common and they may be slow to back down when challenged.

Ascendant in Leo is comfortable with attention and recognition and may engage in self-promotion. They are usually talented and creative, able to take on leadership roles and are often found in charge of whatever operations they may be involved with. Very often they are the first son or daughter born in their family, and consequently strive throughout life to recapture their former favorite status.

Symbol: ♌

Ruling Planet: The Sun.

Body: The heart and spine.

Professions: Owning or managing a business, sales, artistry and musicianship, acting and directing, sports, fashion and entertainment industry work, teaching.

Keywords: Style. Warmth. Dramatic impression. Confidence. Reliable. Royalty. Gold. Creativity. Performance. The personal touch.

Virgo is a sign that is concerned with work, skills, details, and health. People with the Sun in this sign can be proper, meticulous, practical, clinical, materialistic, critical, and fussy. Virgo is a scientific and intellectual sign, emotionally cool, with a tendency to classify and organize things. Work itself is an important issue and there is also a strong service instinct – Virgo often works for others in a specialized or technical service capacity. The Sun in Virgo suggests a sensitive body which often leads to an interest in healing, medicine and diet.

Life Issue: Are things running efficiently?

Moon in Virgo gives an appreciation for competency, cleverness, and craftsmanship. There is usually an interest in physical and mental health, or at least associations with the healing professions. Some can be emotionally cool and very fussy about details and particulars, some may be very clever and insightful.

Ascendant in Virgo types are usually cautious, careful, and even low-key in social situations. They will rarely, or reluctantly, take a strong lead. They are expert with the details, however, and prosper in helping or consulting professions, including education, medicine and law, that require a working knowledge of facts and specifics.

Symbol: ♍

Ruling Planet: Mercury

Body: Intestines, the complexities of digestion

Professions: Service occupations, secretarial work, accounting, legal professions, health or nutrition-related work, crafts, technical work, electronics.

Keywords: Precision. Efficient. Focused on details. Low-risk. Health-conscious. Clever. Sterile. Conservative. Materialistic. Practical. Technical.

Libra, an Air sign, is in many ways the most social of all the signs. The primary motivation for Sun in Libra is human relationships, though this is no guarantee of success in this area. Librans tend to be people-pleasers – friendly, considerate, polite, compromising, and diplomatic. They are also often beauty-conscious, romantic, and flirtatious. The sign is also artistic, sensitive to harmony and balance and requires a calm and peaceful environment to thrive. Decision-making can be a problem, as there is a tendency to look at both sides of an issue very carefully before making any commitment to action.

Life Issue: Let's do it together.

Moon in Libra gives an interest and good taste, in art, music, fashion, and decoration. These are very social people, often very friendly or even flirtatious, who become truly alive only when they are in the company of others. Family is usually an important social outlet for them.

Ascendant in Libra usually produces good-looks, people who dress well and go out of their way to avoid upsets. They are generally eager to please and compromise, at least on the surface. They may also be fond of relaxation and low-energy pursuits. They appreciate the arts and may have very good taste.

Symbol: ♎

Ruling Planet: Venus

Body: Kidneys, lower back

Professions: Social work, counseling, caretaking, public relations, consulting, designing, luxury trades, art, design.

Keywords: Friendly. Harmonious. Balanced. Cooperative. Well-appointed. Soothing. Romantic. Cultured and refined. Relaxed. Lazy.

Scorpio is a Water sign that attempts to be private, but is generally noticed by everyone. Sun in Scorpio types are serious, determined, secretive, strategic, intense, committed, willful, jealous, and sexual. They are usually acutely aware of their placement in a social hierarchy and when at the top may become controlling, even dominating. Scorpio is associated with financial entanglements, the medical field, sex, birth, and death – all of which raise survival issues of a material, psychological, or physical nature. This sign has a direct connection to our most primitive instincts, particularly the reproductive urge, the burrowing or concealing instinct and territorial protection. The Sun in Scorpio gives a strong, resilient body, the ability to focus on a problem and a powerful drive to experience life intensely.

Life Issue: Can I get in any deeper?

Moon in Scorpio gives strong likes and dislikes and an interest in the deeper emotional states of being. This runs from complex relationship entanglements and strong sexual interests to hot, spicy foods. There is also a tendency to fixate intensely on certain things. Often repression and control of strong feelings is needed to manage daily life.

Ascendant in Scorpio suggests a secretive and strategic social personality. Public information about them is usually limited or hard to obtain. There is often an immediate subconscious awareness of the status and intentions of others. Investigating comes naturally to them. Scorpio rising is often perceived by others to exude sexuality.

Symbol: ♏

Ruling Planets: Mars and Pluto.

Body: Sexual and eliminative organs.

Professions: Medicine and healing, surgery, therapy, birthing, aging and dying, psychology, investments, financial work, corporate power, plumbing and wiring, investigative work, the military, sanitation.

Keywords: Depth. Fixations. Focused. Powerful. Primal. Exotic. Sensual. Secretive. Probing. Investigation. Impressive.

Sagittarius is a Fire sign that is usually optimistic, risk-tolerant, sporty, loose and lucky, preferring to experience things first-hand. People with the Sun in Sagittarius generally think big, are intuitive, open-minded, generalizing, playful, generous and positive. There is a tendency to take on more than they can handle resulting in disorder. The sign is associated with extending personal experience through broadening activities like travel, sports, publishing, education, multiculturalism and the understanding of life through philosophy and religion. Religion or morality influences thinking and judgments. Sun in Sagittarius has such a strong liking for freedom that it often resists agreeing to permanent commitments that threaten restrictions. Horses and large dogs are of interest to them.

Life Issue: How much can I bite off?

Moon in Sagittarius gives an interest in literature, outdoor sports, and travel. These are generous people who are not adverse to taking risks. They have a strong love of freedom and will work to create a lifestyle where they can do what they want when they want.

Ascendant in Sagittarius produces a casual and confident personality, one that goes with being an entertainer or teacher. They are explorers and wanderers. The physical build is often tall, or there is an emphasis on the hips and thighs. Some clumsiness and slapdash is common.

Symbol: ♐

Ruling Planet: Jupiter

Body: Hips, thighs, legs, sciatic nerve

Professions: Publishing, traveling, reporting, writing, teaching, law, religion, broadcasting, advertising, sports, politics.

Keywords: Openness. Broad-minded. International. Confident. Generous. Relaxed. Informal. Sporty. Free-wheeling. Generalizing. Slapdash. Varied. Educational.

Capricorn is an Earth sign that is thoughtful, ambitious and typically has achievement of social position as its primary motivation. This may be expressed directly, or indirectly by association. People with the Sun in Capricorn are often hard-working, practical, traditional, materialistic, reliable, persevering, distant, self-disciplined, organized and goal-driven. Being the sign of the father and authority, Capricorn is challenged by issues of responsibility (failure here produces guilt). The sign is quite social and cultured, but conservative and diplomatic; is serious at heart, yet has a sophisticated sense of humor. The leadership style and general social perspective leans towards authoritarian.

Life Issue: Where do I stand relative to others?

Moon in Capricorn gives an interest in business and organization. They strive to be responsible but may have problems with self-control. These are serious people with a need for approval from the public. They have a good business sense and are often successful in the corporate world.

Ascendant in Capricorn produces self-conscious people who are somewhat insecure socially. They often overcompensate for this by taking on responsibilities and management roles. They are generally reliable people who can commit to a project and then deliver it.

Symbol: ♑

Ruling Planet: Saturn

Body: Bones, teeth, joints, knees, hearing.

Professions: Business (executives), organizing, accounting, farming, teaching (college level), mining, administration, government.

Keywords: Formality. Tradition. Professional. Restrained. Self-disciplined. Structured. Serious. Earthy. Geometric. A purist. Critical thinking.

Aquarius is an Air sign that often finds itself holding strongly to intellectual positions that are different from those around them. In general Aquarius leans toward being unconventional, tend to be progressive and sometimes downright weird. People with the Sun in this placement often have strong social motivations and a strong group consciousness, but they don't always fit in with the crowd. Aquarius is about personal freedom and individuality – but how can you really understand these things unless you are part of a group?

Aquarians are rational, inventive, humanitarian, and typically interested in social reforms. This is an intellectual sign, one that can get fixated on ideas to the point of being inflexible. The Aquarian mind works equally well in both scientific and artistic modes.

Life Issue: Why don't I fit in?

The *Moon in Aquarius* gives an interest in the odd, different, and unusual. Topics that interest these people are well off the mainstream and they often become experts in a wayward or arcane subject. What's going on in their emotional life may not concern them, however. They have strong freedom needs, like to be a part of a group, and often have pets or friendships with people unlike themselves.

The *Ascendant in Aquarius* can be friendly, yet emotionally detached. Some have socialization problems and go to extremes one way or another in their social life. Fitting in well with others can be a problem with this rising sign and to others they may appear distant, non-committal or awkward. The commitment to their individuality is strong, but is not always realized without a huge sacrifice.

Symbol: ♒

Ruling Planets: Saturn and Uranus

Body: Ankles, circulation.

Professions: Unusual and self-motivated work, humanitarian work, the social sciences, politics, reformer. inventor, organizations, radio, electronics and computers, aircraft, art, writing.

Keywords: Detached. Unconventional. Maverick. Rigid. Ingenious. Innovative. Progressive. Organizations and groups. Technological.

Pisces, a Water sign, is generally misunderstood by most other people. Sun in Pisces can be highly sensitive, impressionable, psychic, compassionate, and devoted. At best, Pisces thinks big and has a deep understanding of the subtleties of art, science, and religion. At worst, it is confused, hypersensitive and prone to addictions. Pisces types have a strong serving instinct and a willingness to be self-sacrificing for others, or for a cause. It is the sign of institutions such as hospitals and museums – places on the edge of society where individuals become less important than "the mission." On the spiritual level, at least, loss of self seems to be a Piscean goal. Belief can make all the difference with this sign. The Sun in Pisces gives a sensitive body and mind and needs a calm environment in which to flourish.

Life Issue: Why am I here? How can I help?

Moon in Pisces can be escapist, lost in ideas or activities, and not always available to others. There is often an interest in the watery world – the sea, lakes, the rain, and the bathtub. Mysteries and irrational pursuits are appealing. There is usually an interest and talent in performance and the arts, especially music, theater, and dance.

Ascendant in Pisces produces a very adaptable personality, but one that is also extremely sensitive to the environment. These types need to be around calm people in calm situations, otherwise they may soak up too much tense or negative energy. The sense of self is not very strong with this rising sign and long periods of privacy may be needed to balance out the influences of the world.

Symbol: ♓

Ruling Planet: Jupiter and Neptune

Body: Feet and lymphatic system.

Professions: Non-profit work, service occupations, nursing, healing, and hospital work, secretarial work, cleaning, dancing, the arts, work with liquids (paint, alcohol, water, etc.), research, religion.

Keywords: Mysterious. Impressionistic. Artistic-bohemian. Chaotic. Escape. Denial. Spiritual. Camouflage. Intangible. Soft. The sea, fish and ships. The color purple. Clouds.

Affinities with the Planets

Although the Sun's seasonal cycle defines the signs of the zodiac, the Moon and planets pass through them as well. Traditionally, each planet was said to have a special affinity or resonance with particular signs. These linkages between the signs and the planets, called rulerships, follow a symmetrical pattern. Arranging the signs with the Cancer-Leo cusp at the center, the Sun and Moon rule Leo and Cancer respectively, Mercury, the next planet, rules the next two signs on either side, Virgo and Gemini. Venus rules Libra and Taurus, the next two signs. Mars rules Scorpio and Aries, Jupiter rules Sagittarius and Pisces, and Saturn rules Capricorn and Aquarius. Note that this order is the same order as planets arranged by their distance from the Sun. Note also that, except for the Sun and Moon, each planet rules one masculine sign and one feminine sign. This perfect symmetry, sometimes called the "ladder of the planets" was challenged when Uranus, Neptune and Pluto were discovered in the 18th, 19th, and 20th centuries. These outer planets are now regarded as additional, higher-octave rulers of three of the social signs. Uranus is thought to be a co-ruler of Aquarius, Neptune a co-ruler of Pisces and Pluto a co-ruler of Scorpio.

Signs of the Zodiac

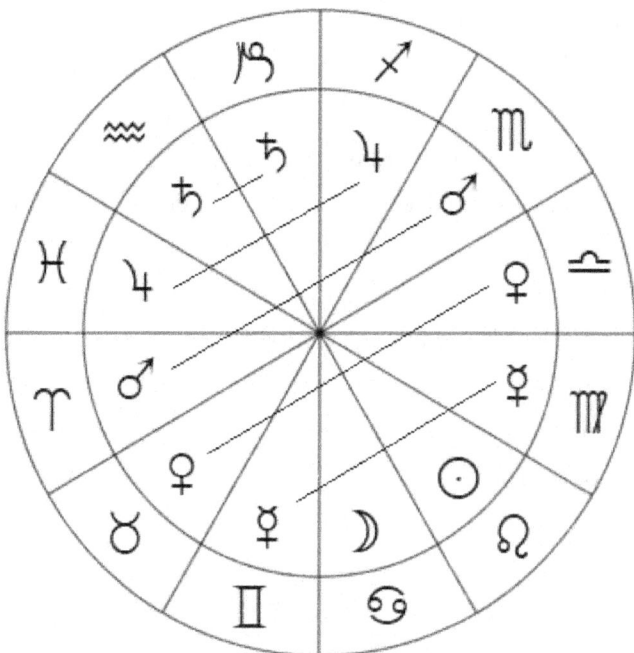

Figure 6. Planetary Affinity

Dignities and Debilities

In addition to being the ruler or lord of one or two zodiacal signs, the planets are said to have specific relationships with other signs, and portions of signs, as well. The basic idea is that some signs are very conducive to the energies projected by a planet while other aren't. For example let's consider Mercury, the planet of thought, speech, and communication. It makes perfect sense that Mercury would function best in signs that support rational thought and communication. Very logically, Mercury rules Gemini and Virgo as these signs are concerned with thought and movement. But put Mercury in Pisces, a sign that is weak on boundaries, sensitive and emotional, and it may not be able to express itself so well. A similar situation is found when Mercury is in Sagittarius, a sign that takes in a lot of information and generalizes.

In the table below are four traditional categories for the planets as they relate to the signs: rulership, detriment, exaltation and fall. If you look at this table carefully you'll see it makes perfect sense and can serve as a guide to how planets may hold to their basic principles yet differ in certain ways. In the classical astrology of Rome, the Middle Ages and the Renaissance this table of dignities and debilities also includes three other categories: triplicity, term and face. Together, these are known as the *Essential Dignities*, information on which can be easily found online or in books. Notice that in the table below, the additional modern rulers of Scorpio, Aquarius and Pisces are noted as well, but because these planets were discovered in modern times, there is as of yet no general agreement on their other placements in the scheme of dignities.

SIGN	RULER	DETRIMENT	EXALTATION	FALL
Aries	Mars	Venus	Sun	Saturn
Taurus	Venus	Mars	Moon	
Gemini	Mercury	Jupiter		
Cancer	Moon	Saturn	Jupiter	Mars
Leo	Sun	Saturn		
Virgo	Mercury	Jupiter	Mercury	Venus
Libra	Venus	Mars	Saturn	Sun
Scorpio	Mars/Pluto	Venus		Moon
Sagittarius	Jupiter	Mercury		
Capricorn	Saturn	Moon	Mars	Jupiter
Aquarius	Saturn/Uranus	Sun		
Pisces	Jupiter/Neptune	Mercury	Venus	Mercury

7

Houses: Sectors of Sky

The planets in an astrological chart are positioned in both zodiacal signs and within sectors of the sky called houses or domiciles. Signs are a scale for measuring where a planet is located in space, from the perspective of an observer on Earth. Houses are a scale for measuring where a planet is located in its daily (diurnal) cycle that is driven by the rotation of the Earth. This is the cycle of rising to setting, and then back to rising again that is completed each day by the Sun, Moon and the planets. Houses also tell where a planet is from the standpoint of a particular place on Earth. They will reveal if a planet is above or below the horizon, and if it is rising, passing overhead, setting, or passing underfoot on the other side of the Earth.

Houses make information about daily risings and settings even more specific by dividing the space surrounding a given point on Earth into twelve sectors. If you are in the northern hemisphere, imagine you are looking at the sky and facing south (see diagram below). The sun will rise to your left on the eastern horizon and set to your right on the western horizon. As you can see in the diagram below, the horizon is the Ascendant-Descendant axis. At sunrise, the Sun is on the Ascendant, and it enters the 12th house just after sunrise. About midway between sunrise and noon it would be in the 11th house; approaching noon (as it is in the diagram) it would be in the 10th house; just after noon it would be in the ninth; and so forth, through a 24-hour period until the Sun rises again. The Moon and planets make the same daily progress up in the sky and then down again, each at its own times of day depending on where it happens to be in the zodiac relative to the Sun. In the diagram below, the Moon has already risen and is in the 12th house, and a star has recently set and is invisible as it passes under Earth. It is located on the cusp of the 6th house.

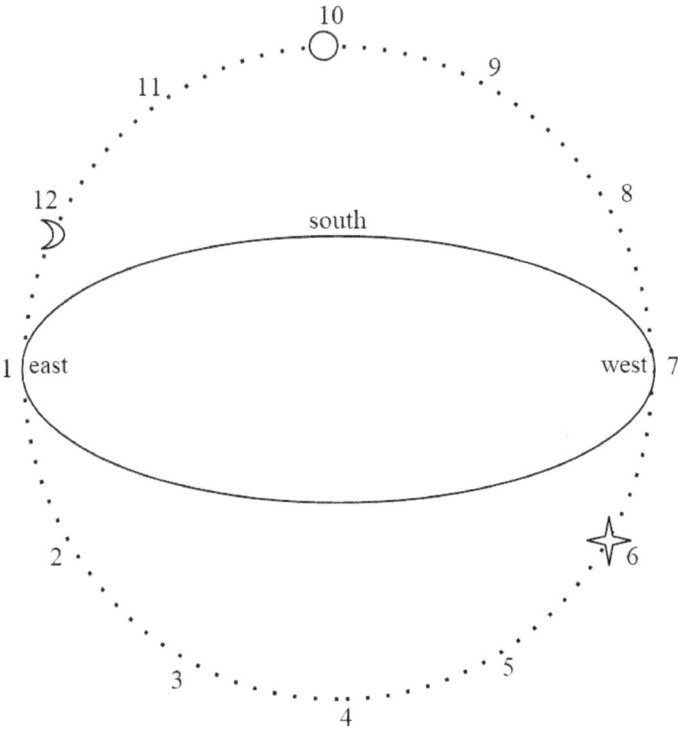

Figure 7. Daily Rising and Setting

Considering this clockwise daily motion of the planets, you might ask why the houses are numbered counterclockwise. This is probably because ancient astrologers thought of the twelve houses as analogous to the twelve signs. In fact, as we shall see further on, there is some symbolic similarity between the first house and the first sign, the second house and the second sign, etc. Unlike the signs, however, houses can be more or less than 30 degrees in length. This is due to geometrical complexities, and it gets more pronounced the further north or south a birth is from the Earth's equator. The exact width of a house also depends on which of the dozens of methods of house division an astrologer uses.

The Ascendant and MC Axes

Understanding the framework of the astrological chart is important as it connects chart interpretation with the realities of the sky on the day of a birth or event. How the sky is charted is a subject in itself usually referred to as coordinate systems, a subtopic within astronomy. Astrology uses the astronomical data from coordinate systems which it then interprets. In astrology, it is a framework based on the horizon and the meridian that make up the cross on which the daily motions of the planets are positioned. This framework is the astrological chart. The next section may seem abstract, and it is, but once understood it organizes everything in a chart. The starting point of an astrological chart has always been the Ascendant, the point in the east that is rising as Earth rotates.

The Ascendant is the point where the ecliptic or Sun's path intersects the horizon in the east. Planets rise near the Ascendant and set near the Descendant. (The Ascendant is also known as the Rising Sign.) Traditionally, the Ascendant was called the horoscope – it was literally the "view of the hour". At 180 degrees opposite to the Ascendant, at the other end of the horizon axis, is the Descendant, where the ecliptic intersects the horizon in the west. Taken together, the Ascendant and Descendant form the horizon, or Ascendant/Descendant axis of the astrological chart. In most methods of house division, these two points mark the cusps of the first and seventh houses. While there are many ways of dividing the chart into twelve houses, there is no dispute about where the Ascendant/Descendant is located. These two points create a primary division of the sky into night and day that is the framework of an astrological chart. The Ascendant and Descendant divide the sky into two hemispheres: one above and the other below the horizon.

The MC or MC (abbreviation of medium coeli, "middle heaven" in Latin) is the point where the Sun's path (ecliptic) intersects the meridian, a great circle in the sky that runs due north and south (directly over the Earth's north and south poles). The MC is where the Sun is located at approximately noon; this is the highest position of a planet in its daily cycle when seen from a particular spot on Earth. The IC (abbreviated from imum coeli, or "lowest heaven") is 180 degrees opposite the MC; it is the lowest a planet goes in its daily cycle and where the Sun is located at midnight. The IC is actually located beneath the observer on the other side of the Earth. Together, the MC and IC form the meridian axis of the astrological chart. This cross-like axis divides the sky, and the astrological chart, into two other hemispheres: eastern and western. The MC and IC are usually the cusps of the tenth and fourth houses.

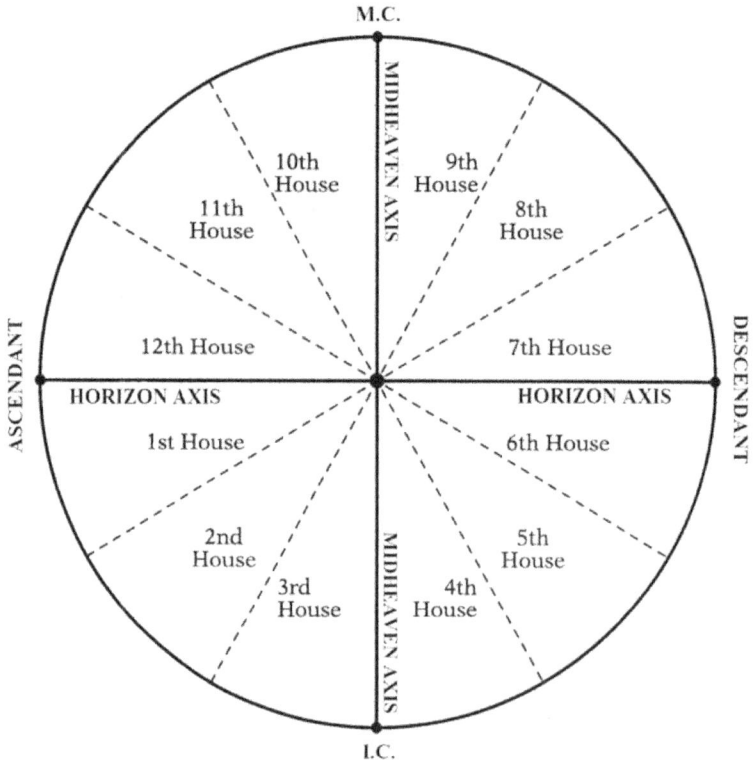

Figure 8. Angles of the Chart

Because the ecliptic, the Sun's path, is tilted about 23 degrees with respect to the Earth's equator, the Ascendant and MC are not always 90 degrees from each other. Rather, their angular relationship changes in the course of the day and is different at different latitudes on Earth. The Ascendant, Descendant, MC and IC are powerful points in their own right, and they are also the cusps of the 1st, 7th, 10th, and 4th houses in most house systems. They also represent the four cardinal directions (east, west, south, and north) and are called the "angles" of the astrological chart. The Gauquelin statistical studies (described in Chapter 1) have provided evidence supporting the importance of these angles. If a planet is near the Ascendant, MC, Descendant or IC, its qualities will tend to manifest strongly in the life of the individual. The Gauquelin studies found that planets near the Ascendant or MC tend to be a bit stronger than those near the Descendant or IC. Astrologers have also found that planets in aspect to one of these points tend to assume importance in the chart, particularly the hard 90-degree, 45-degree, and 135-degree aspects. Along with the Sun and Moon, the Ascendant and MC are the most important points in the astrological chart.

House Systems

The Ascendant-Descendant axis divides the chart into upper and lower hemispheres, so that planets are defined as being either above the horizon or below it. The MC– IC axis divides the chart into eastern and western hemispheres, with planets that are on their way up and those that are on their way down. These four angles of the astrological chart divide the chart into four quadrants. Further division of these quadrants into three sections each is the basis for most of the numerous methods of house division. (A few methods use only the Ascendant or MC as reference points.) In general, however, with only slight differences, all house systems measure where the planets are in their daily cycle around the Earth.

The beginnings or "cusps" of the first, fourth, seventh and tenth houses are not usually a matter of dispute because they coincide with the angles (Ascendant, Descendant, MC, IC). Most astrologers take these cusps quite seriously if they are sure the birth time is reasonably accurate. The cusps of the other houses (two, three, five, six, eight, nine, eleven, and twelve) can be different depending on the house method used. Many astrologers regard these intermediate house cusps as only approximate; a planet near the end of one house is thought by many astrologers to partake somewhat of the qualities of the next house. Today, most English-speaking astrologers use the Placidus or Koch house systems; others use Equal houses (30-degree sections) starting at the Ascendant, or Whole Sign houses (also 30-degree sections) that start from the first degree of the sign that the Ascendant is in. In Europe you might hear more about Regiomontanus houses; siderealists use Campanus houses; and in India, Porphyry houses are used. Dozens of methods of house division exist: this is one area in astrology on which there has never been much agreement.

What the Houses Show

Whereas the fastest-moving solar system body, the Moon, takes a month to go around the zodiac, and Saturn takes 29 years to do the same, the planets take only 24 hours to go through all the houses. The houses, which are an effect of the rotation of the Earth, are thus the fastest-moving part of the astrological chart. The degree of the zodiac that marks the beginning of a house advances on the average of one degree for every four minutes of time. Therefore, to erect an astrological chart with accurate houses, we need to know the exact time of day that a person was born. Also, the houses represent how the heavens look from a particular spot on Earth. Two people born at the same time may have planets in the same degrees of the zodiac, but, unless they are born very close to each other geographically, their Ascendant, MC, and intermediate house cusps will be different. This is the reason astrologers need also to know the latitude and longitude at which a person was born.

Time and geographical variables make houses an element of the astrological chart that best describe an individual's particular circumstances in life. Two people born on the same day but at different times may have similar underlying motivations, as shown by the relationships of the planets in the zodiac. But the way these motivations find their outlet in daily life is shown by the houses which can be dramatically different in the charts of births separated by just a few minutes.

In astrological interpretation, the houses are used to determine the kinds of experiences that are most natural, appropriate, and likely to occur for the individual in each of the various areas of the life. First, the house in which a planet is located shows the area of life in which that planet's influence is most likely to manifest. Second, the sign on the beginning or cusp of a house also indicates to the astrologer how the area of life associated with that house will tend to operate. Third, the planet that is the ruler of the sign on the cusp of a house may also be a key to how that house will work in a life and its zodiacal position needs to be noted. Fourth, a planet that is in close aspect to a house ruler will translate its effects to that house.[13] House interpretation is complex and there are many traditional methodologies that are routinely employed in the investigation of an astrological chart.

Meanings of the Houses

1. The *first house* extends from the Ascendant (the cusp of the first house) to about thirty degrees below the horizon. The Ascendant was originally called the horoscope, Greek for "hour view." This definition says much about the importance of precise timing when interpreting an astrological chart. Unfortunately, the term has been misapplied and has distorted the public's understanding of astrology. The Ascendant point itself symbolizes the mask, persona, or presentation of self in the social world. Like the Ascendant, the

---

13   For example, suppose the 2nd house is unoccupied but Aries is on the cusp, and Mars, being the ruler of Aries, is found in the 4th house in Gemini. Further, Mars is in conjunction with Saturn. It will then be Saturn, coming from the 4th house, that gets translated via Mars to the 2nd house and this would imply difficulties and delays in achieving financial success that are anchored in matters of parents, family, home, and territory.

space designated by the first house also has much to do with the social identity and personality. Traditionally, it is said to define the natural self-expression, the physical body and appearance, mannerisms, temperament, and social attitudes. It also symbolizes self-awareness and the assertion of self.

2. The *second house* symbolizes one's economic circumstances, abilities to generate income and also the skills and talents we have that are worth something in a practical sense. It shows our resources, ownership, money, and possessions.

3. The *third house* traditionally rules information, messaging, communication devices, correspondence, neighbors, siblings, relatives, local mobility, and the local environment. It has to do with both the nature of our immediate environment, social and physical, and how we navigate it and might best come to terms with it.

4. The *fourth house* rules the domestic home, the base of operations, parents, family, the ancestral tradition or roots, property, territory and internal personal security. It symbolizes the very personal and emotional experience of centering and securing oneself in the world.

5. The *fifth house* is the area of self-enhancement, personal expression, usually expressed through children, artistic creativity, risk-taking and game-playing. This house rules salesmanship, "show business," love affairs, and courtship – all a kind of performance.

6. The *sixth house* is about work, crises, and adjustments, and says much about the daily routine and schedule. The mastery of specific techniques and service to others are also themes. It is also the house of mental and physical health – our challenges and ability to make things (including the body) run smoothly and efficiently.

7. The *seventh house* indicates significant others, marriage, business partnerships, and other one-to-one relationships. It has to do with awareness

of others in general, their natures and intentions, and also with the prospects and potentials for participation and cooperation with them. It also indicates open enemies, those with whom we openly compete.

8. The *eighth house* is the area of shared resources, of materials that are jointly owned or are used with other people. It covers inheritances and trusts, and any other type of financial entanglement such as investments, loans, debts, and lotteries. It is associated with emotional entanglement as well – shared rituals, including reunions, which function to revitalize relationships. Challenges in regard to trust, a necessary ingredient in sexual matters and in sustaining relationships, is shown here. The eighth house is the house of divorce, crisis, mystery, occultism, and death and the beyond.

9. The *ninth house* provides information about the search for meaning in life. It is associated with travel, education, religion, higher knowledge, philosophy, law, and deep mental comprehension. Promotion, publishing, and advertising, which involve extending ideas to many minds, all come under its rule.

10. The *tenth house* usually begins at the MC which, like the Ascendant, is in itself a very important personal point in the birth-chart. The tenth house has to do with life direction and career. It shows our vocation or calling in life, our reputation and status. It is our public persona and shows how we fit into our community. Like the fourth house, the tenth house is also associated with parents.

11. The *eleventh house* describes the social world we find ourselves in. It rules friends, groups, associations, and organizations. It symbolizes our activities within social units, our social aspirations, and the values held by our friends and peers.

12. The *twelfth house* rules privacy, deep insights and investigations. It is the area of hidden or secret things, psychic experiences, working behind the scenes, spirituality, illumination, personal sacrifice, karma, solitude,

and confinement (sometimes the result of failing to conform to the rules or rituals of institutions or belief systems). It symbolizes powers greater than the self, such as institutions and belief systems. The twelfth house is also the house of vision and cosmic perspective, but also of failures and defeats and how we deal with them.

A Personal Zodiac

As mentioned above, the houses are boundaries that chart the daily cycle of planetary risings and settings from a particular point on Earth. Houses are sometimes thought of as kind of personal zodiac, somewhat parallel to the signs in meaning. For example, connections can be made between the first house and the first sign, Aries. People with many planets in the first house may be very self-absorbed, as are those with many planets in Aries. Many fashion models have Venus in the first house, their physical appearance being the most important element in their lives. Planets in the second house are, like planets in Taurus, related to money and resources. The third house, like Gemini, involves learning, talking, and visiting neighbors. In the fourth house, as in Cancer, emotional matters, home, family, nesting, and nurturing are major themes. Leo corresponds to the fifth house, which has to do with performance and creativity. People often have children when major planets transit the fifth house. The sixth house has to do with work, health, schedules, etc., much like Virgo.

The next six houses follow the same pattern. The seventh house is, like Libra, associated with relationships, particularly partnerships and marriages. The eighth house is like Scorpio in that the issues are sex, death, trust, and sharing. The ninth house, which indicates travel, learning and legal matters, can be linked to Sagittarius. Capricorn and the tenth house rule honor, status and reputation. Aquarius and the eleventh house show friends, groups, and other social associations. Pisces and the twelfth house are both linked with the unfinished, the complex and the unseen.

Houses: Sectors of Sky

While they share some common themes, signs and houses serve different functions in the chart. Signs are more like adjectives that further color or qualify the planets. Planets will express their basic nature better in some signs than others. If a planet is in the sign it rules, for example Venus in Taurus, it is traditionally said to have dignity. Likewise, certain signs may work against a planets, this being called debility. A complex schemata that lists the different combinations planet and sign is called a table of essential dignities (see Chapter 4). Houses, on the other hand, show the particular departments of life in which a planet is likely to have its strongest influence. Houses show where (in life) the planets operate; signs show how they express. Some house positions are better for planets than others and when placed in these the planet is said to have accidental dignity.

The Planets in the Houses

Each planet has its own particular effect on the matters indicated by the house in which it is located. Many planets in a house indicate an emphasis on the matters of that house; more than one trend may be discernible. The natural trend of a house's particular area of life is also symbolized by the zodiacal sign on the house cusp, especially when there are no planets in that house.

The Sun gives great emphasis to the house where it is located. There is a need to center the life around that house's issues, consciously working and growing those issues so that they will be strong and well-defined. For example, with the Sun in the third house, there would be a need to focus on relatives, siblings, neighbors and matters of communication and transportation. Focusing on the issues of the house the Sun is in can improve self-worth and overall life integration and can assist in career-related matters.

The Moon suggests that matters of the house it falls in are likely to be reactive, affected by emotions and moods, and characterized by fluctuations and frequent changes. Matters of the house are then often best approached intuitively.

Mercury in a house indicates informational activity, discussion and commerce in regard to its matters. This pronounced mental or communicative tendency suggests that challenges regarding the house's subject matter are best handled rationally and not impulsively.

Venus emphasizes the need to relate to others in regard to the specific matters of the house it is in. It also calls for a consideration of the emotional aspects of the area of life indicated by its house position and the value of compromise. Venus also stimulates the desire nature in regard to the things of the house, and generally brings rewards.

Mars suggests the need to take action or be constructive in regard to a house's subject matter. This can be activity, competition or conflict. It symbolizes both strife and a need to take initiative in the matters ruled by the house in which it is located.

Jupiter brings optimism, confidence, growth and luck, usually making its house a noticeably successful area of life. However, there may also be a tendency to be overly optimistic or generous in regard to the matters of the house it is in, a condition that could be problematic. Judgments, acted on in the context of a guiding philosophy or religion, may affect the matters of the house Jupiter is in.

Saturn indicates the matters of the house need to be approached consciously and logically. These matters can be prone to delays and problems, which require patience, discipline, and organization to solve them. Saturn puts limits on what is possible in that house and challenges one to work harder to compensate.

Uranus tends to disrupt the matters of its house position and suggests erratic and unstable patterns and a need for spontaneity and experimentation. Lack of continuity and reversals in the house's subject matter favor living more in the present and being flexible.

Neptune suggests blind spots and a tendency to dwell on ideals or the future. The areas of life indicated by its house position need to be handled intuitively, creatively, and sensitively. There is a need to recognize the limits of control over circumstances in the house's subject matter and learn to know when to trust and when not to.

Pluto indicates entanglements and complications involving others in regard to the house's subject matter. It also suggests the need for exploration and investigation of the themes of the house it is in and it also often subjects these matters to shocks and deep transformations. Pluto intensifies matters and suggests the need for new beginnings and favors change and turnovers.

The astrological chart

Having outlined planets, aspects, signs and houses, we are now ready to show how they all interact in a astrological chart. The chart itself is basically a map of the sky calculated for the time and place of an event. It is a time-slice, a frame of the moving sky captured in a diagram. The convention in Western astrology has always been to map the sky as it appears if one were facing south with east to the left and west to the right. From this position the Sun, Moon and planets will be seen to rise in the east, culminate at the MC and then set in the west. The figure below depicts a moment frozen in time when the planet Mars was rising in the east but very close to the Ascendant, where the zodiac meets the horizon. Pluto was already above the horizon, and Jupiter and Moon, in conjunction, were headed towards setting. The other planets were only visible on the other side of the Earth.

What Astrology is ...And How to Use it

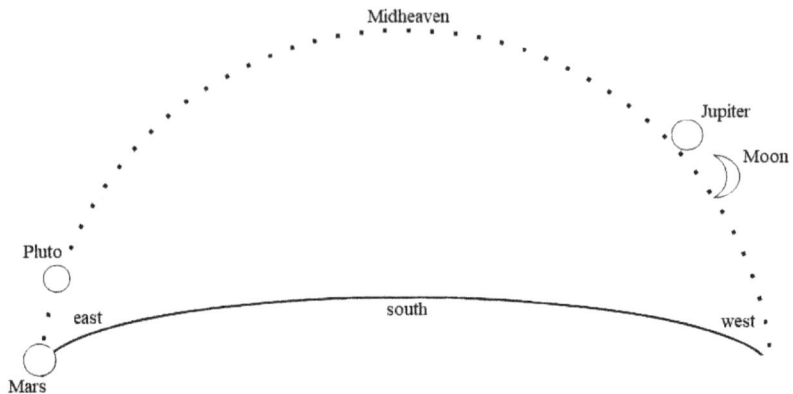

Figure 9. Astrolocal Chart. Here is the sky facing south with planets rising in the east and setting in the west. The solid line is the horizon, the dotted line is the ecliptic (path of the Sun) which is normally divided into zodiacal signs not shown here.

Most astrologers use astrological charts, essentially more complex versions of the figure above, that capture the paths of the planets as they move through the sky. These charts are typically circular in form like the one shown below. In the astrological chart, the houses are noted by sign, degree, and minute. In the chart below, the Ascendant, or cusp of the first house, is 25 degrees 34 minutes of Scorpio (25♏34). Each planet is located in a house and is indicated by its symbol or glyph, along with the degrees and minutes of its sign position. The resulting diagram or map of the sky, what some call the astrological chart wheel, gives us the main information needed to interpret the chart. As you can see here, the Sun in Sagittarius was below the horizon but in the first house; the person was born about two hours before sunrise. Notice that five planets are located in the second house which must certainly complicate issues related to finances and resources. This is the astrological chart of Taylor Swift. Compare this chart with Figure 9 above and you'll see that Mars is very close to the Ascendant, Pluto has already risen and Jupiter and the Moon, both in the sign Cancer and positioned in the eighth house, are moving towards setting. The conjunction of the Moon and Jupiter has always been considered an indication of confidence and good fortune.

Houses: Sectors of Sky

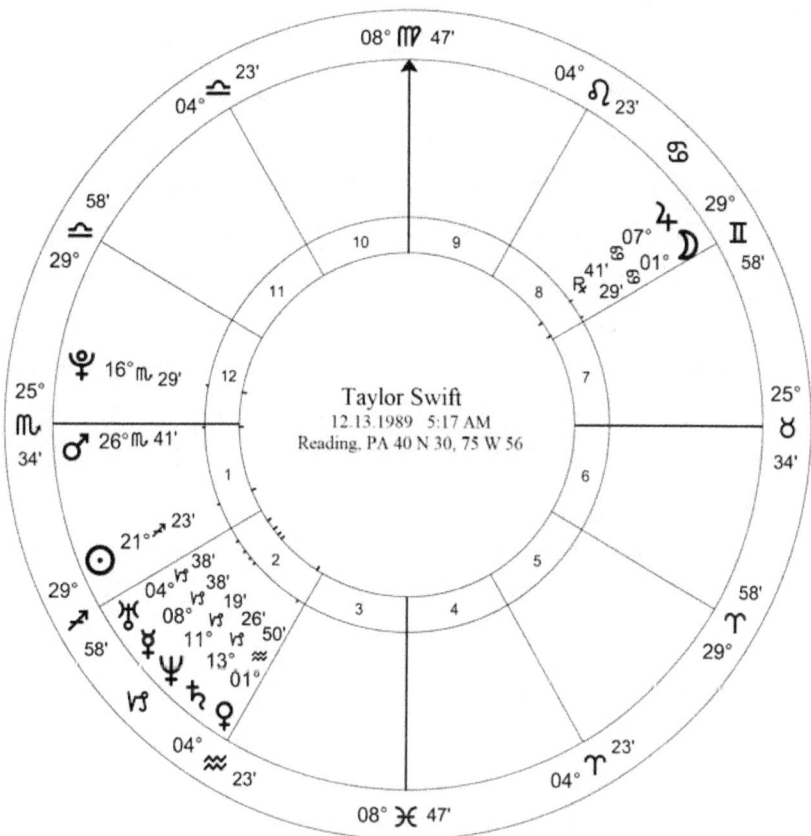

Figure 10. Taylor Swift

Hemisphere Emphasis

As noted earlier, the Ascendant – Descendant axis, which lies across the horizon from east to west, divides the sky that is visible from the part of the sky that the observer cannot see. In Taylor Swift's chart the Ascendant – Descendant axis is shown by the horizontal line at the beginning of the first house in the east and the beginning of the seventh house in the west (25 Scorpio to 25 Taurus). Notice that her chart has seven planets below this dividing line – Mars, Sun, Uranus, Mercury, Neptune, Saturn and Venus.

113

Only Pluto, Jupiter and the Moon were above the horizon and potentially visible at the time of her birth.

The hemisphere above the horizon, the upper hemisphere, is concerned with the outer world, the world of participation and social mixing. These are houses 7 through 12. People who have most or all of their planets in this hemisphere are motivated by the ways of the world. They live in a consensus reality that is constructed by people in the world. Two good examples of this are a scientist who seeks agreement from others in regard to a finding she has made. Science is a collective activity and those who do science participate with others to discover common truths. Another example would be a politician who, in seeking supporters, strives to walk a middle path so as to be appealing to a majority. In both of these cases it is the objective social world that is focused on.

The hemisphere below the horizon, the lower hemisphere designated by houses 1 through 6, is very different and concerned with what a person feels and knows on their own terms. People with most or all planets in this hemisphere are motivated by feelings and desires. An example would be a person who is a homebody, rarely traveling and keeping close to family. Another example is a person in the restaurant or hotel business, these being temporary "homes" where people come to visit or stay. Poets are moved by their own feelings and experiences and give these to the world in verse. The very religious likewise draw on their own inner world view and often attempt to convert others to their perspectives and beliefs. In all cases, these people are focused on their subjective reality as a primary motivator.

The circle of sky around us can also be divided into two hemispheres using the axis formed by the MC and the IC. Here the eastern hemisphere is the space designated by houses 10-12 and 1-3, with the Ascendant in the middle. This hemisphere is the zone of self-interest and self-reliance. People with the majority of planets in this hemisphere are self-starters and build on themselves. In general they are less reliant on others and prefer to do things on their own terms. The western hemisphere is designated by houses

4 through 9, with the Descendant in the middle. People with most or all of their planets in this hemisphere are more reliant on others and more inclined to form relationships, partner with others or work closely with people.

Relocating the Houses: Astro-Mapping

A birth occurs at a specific instant in time – but where this birth occurs on the globe can make a difference. A birth occurring at 10 AM in New York City would occur when the Sun was well up into the sky, probably in the eleventh house of the birth chart for this moment. At this same instant in Los Angeles, which is three times zones west, or three hours earlier, the Sun was just rising and in either the first or twelfth house. In Hawaii, another two hours earlier, the Sun had not yet risen and wouldn't for several hours.

Astrologers have found that when people move away from their birth place, they become sensitive to a chart calculated for their instant of birth, but at their new location. The zodiacal positions of the planets in the new (relocated) chart remain the same as the birth chart, but the house positions change, and this factor can alter the planetary emphasis. Exactly where on Earth these planetary shifts occur can be plotted on a map. The use of these maps can give an interesting perspective on the potential effects of a relocation. In many cases people experience very noticeable changes in their lives when they move to a place where planets occupy different houses, even more so when planets are exactly conjunct the Ascendant, Descendant, MC or IC. Such reconfigurations, depending on the planets, may improve their life or bring different challenges. This technique is called astro-mapping or astro*carto*graphy.

8

Reading a Birth Chart

The art of interpreting a birth chart requires a thorough knowledge of astrological symbols, extensive experience, and good judgment. Teaching this skill is well beyond the scope of this book. Still, anyone with some patience, common sense, and an understanding of astrological symbolism can learn how to extract valuable and accurate information from a chart that will set the foundations for more complex analysis. This chapter provides an overview of how an astrological interpretation proceeds. A number of standard techniques and methodologies will be presented in a simple form along with easy ways to apply them. In describing each of these methods an example chart, shown below, will be used.

At its best, the interpretive reading of a birth chart is a revealing, useful, and insightful narrative assembled from an analysis of astrological symbols. The reading could be short and only superficially descriptive, or it could be hours long and delve deeply into a life history, locate in time transformative life events past and future and, of course, analyze the complex behavior patterns and attitudes that make up a personality. All of these dimensions of a life can be discovered in a birth chart by an experienced practitioner. Reaching such a level of interpretation, however, requires much experience as well as considerable knowledge of other subjects relating to human nature. A good astrologer is like a competent physician or psychologist who brings many years of work and much accumulated knowledge to the table. That being said, a few basic techniques useful for reading a chart, ones that anyone can do, are offered here.

Reading a Birth Chart

A good place to start a reading, whether it be long or short, is to consider what might be called the big three personality centers: the Ascendant, Moon and Sun. In many ways these are the most important focal points in an astrological chart and just their positions by sign and house alone will say much about a person. The Ascendant describes the social identity, the presentation of self, how a person comes across to other people and the world in general. The Moon describes a person's natural skills and abilities, and their interests. The Sun says much about purpose, central life concerns, personal strength, and leadership style. In the example chart below we see that the Sun is in Leo, the Moon in Gemini and Aquarius is on the Ascendant.

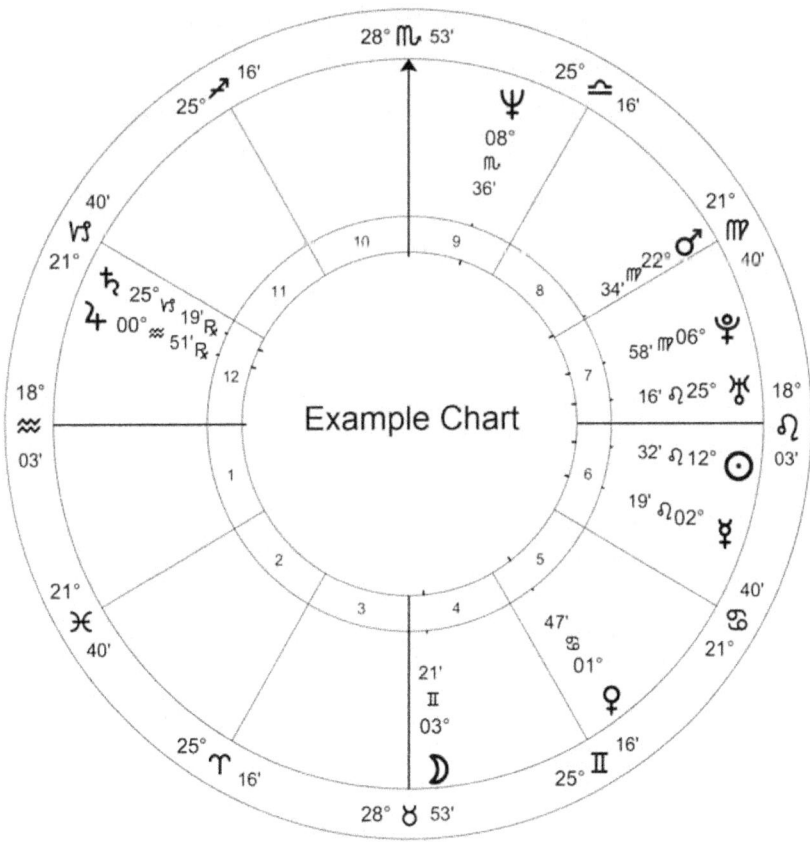

Figure 11. Example chart

The Ascendant in this chart (at 9-o'clock on the wheel) is in Aquarius, located at just over 18 degrees of that sign. With the Ascendant in Aquarius, this person identifies as different, perhaps even as an outsider. Aquarius suggests that this person is probably very socially-inclined and progressive, but they also display personal quirks and some rigidities. With the Moon in Gemini, this person is probably thoughtful, has natural communication skills, is open to many subjects and ideas and is intellectually flexible and willing to learn. With the Sun in Leo, this person has natural leadership abilities and is most comfortable when at the center of things. This person may be creative or have a natural dramatic flair. By elaborating on these three points, which requires a good understanding of the signs and points themselves, a lot of information can be extracted from the chart. If these signs and points are well understood in principle, the simple synthesis of just these three points can serve as a core from which much information can be built on. The way to learn this kind of synthesis is to start simple. Below is a table that reduces these three personal points to a short sentence made by filling in the blanks with the appropriate words from the list.

You are a (Ascendant) who (Moon) for the purpose of (Sun).

SIGN	ASCENDANT	MOON	SUN
Aries	soloist	responds rapidly	autonomy
Taurus	steady worker	gains assets	security
Gemini	communicator	manages information	communication
Cancer	caretaker	displays sensitivity	preservation
Leo	creator	teaches	leadership
Virgo	perfectionist	engages details	perfection
Libra	socializer	builds harmony	cooperation
Scorpio	investigator	has passion	strength
Sagittarius	freelancer	generalizes	perspective
Capricorn	diplomat	works hard	control
Aquarius	outsider	seeks novelty	individuality
Pisces	dreamer	serves others	the greater good

In the sample chart used this sentence would be "You are an <u>outsider</u> who <u>manages information</u> for the purpose of <u>leadership</u>."

This approach to blending symbols, in this case three, is a model for further interpretation of a chart. The more one understands the Ascendant, Moon and Sun, and the zodiacal signs, the more sentences can be generated. The same method can be used with planets in signs and houses. For example, an interpretation of Mars in Gemini in the seventh house needs to first consider what Mars means (force, energy, competition) in its sign (Gemini = communications) and house (house 7 = partners, others). Here one could say that others communicate with power, a general statement that implies tough negotiations or arguments with a spouse or partner. Or significant others express themselves with force. While this approach appears simplistic, it does give the interpretive process a starting point. As with anything else, good results come with experience.

The next step in evaluating a chart is to look for any angular planets, that is the conjunction of any planet with the angles of the astrological chart; the Ascendant, MC, Descendant, or IC. As noted before, angular planets tend to be far more powerful than planets located elsewhere. In fact, planets within roughly seven degrees of an angle are usually the most powerful planets in the chart.[14] The "angularity" of any planet will suggest much about how the person experiences life and interacts with others. For example, when Saturn is angular, the personality tends to be cautious; when Mars is angular, the personality tends to have a high tolerance for risk. It is this type of effect which has been proven statistically by the Gauquelins. In the example chart, both the Sun and Moon are close to the Descendant and IC respectively. This is an indicator of a strong personality.

Other important considerations include the most elevated planet and the Ascendant ruler. The planet that is highest in the sky in a chart (the most elevated planet) should be accorded some extra value. The most elevated

---

14   Many astrologers extend this boundary to 15 degrees or more.

planet could be anywhere above the horizon, depending on the chart, but it may be particularly strong if it is located (as the Gauquelin studies found) close to the MC In the example chart above, Neptune is the most elevated planet, in this case located in the 9th house. Being the planet of ideals and visions, this would suggest a person who embodies an ideal, tells a story, and is a dreamer or visionary – or all of the above.

The planet that rules the sign on the Ascendant also has more power or significance. In the example above, the Ascendant is in Aquarius. The traditional ruler of Aquarius is Saturn, though in modern times many also consider Uranus to be the co-ruler. This suggests both should be looked at carefully when interpreting the chart. In the example, Uranus is in Leo and Saturn is in Capricorn, both signs of leadership and organization. Notice that these two form a quincunx aspect, an indication of tradeoffs and having to settle. The only other signs with modern co-rulers are Scorpio (Mars/Pluto) and Pisces (Jupiter/Neptune), the others will have only one planetary ruler.

The general distribution of planets in a chart is very important and will reveal any hemisphere emphasis. There is considerable difference between charts with the majority of planets clustered in the eastern part of the sky (left side of the chart) and those with a dominant western hemisphere. In the example chart, more planets are located in the western hemisphere. This suggests that social relations and compromises are primary themes. Similarly, a majority of planets located above the horizon contrast with those who have a majority below. In the example, a majority above suggests a more public life. The sign positions of the planets are also very important and tell much about general orientations in life. From the elements, qualities and polarities of the signs we can know more about how the planets in total function in a chart. How to use this information with a weighted scoring system will be described below.

What psychologists look for

Before going further into astrological interpretation, let's consider what it is we hope to find in a chart that can be categorized as personality. The field of psychology has been studying personality for many years but is still far from offering a complete explanation. Typically, information about personality is built around models, most of them simple and quite limited. One popular model is the Myers-Briggs personality type indicator (MBTI) which is based on Jung's four functions (intuition, sensation, thinking and feeling) and the two orientations extraversion and introversion. It is a fact that Jung studied astrology and derived the functions from the four elements (Fire, Earth, Air and Water). Likewise, the two orientations are like the sign polarities. To Jung's classifications Myers and Briggs added two more functions, judging and perceiving, which refer more to orientation to the outer world and the process of decision making. All these categories are viewed as on scale with extremes where most people fall somewhere in between. A total of 16 possible personality "types" are generated by this model.

Extraversion (+ polarity) is preference to deal directly with the outer world and its people, things, and situations.

Introversion (− polarity) is preference to deal more directly with the inner world and ideas, information, beliefs and explanations.

Sensing (Earth) is dealing with facts, what is known, the physical sensations and striving for clarity.

Intuition (Fire) is dealing with ideas, looking into the unknown, grasping new possibilities and seeing what isn't obvious.

Thinking (Air) is being analytical, detached and making decisions on the basis of rational thought and objective logic.

Feeling (Water) is using felt values and what or who you believe is important in making decisions.

Judgment (Saturn?) is preferring life to be planned and structured.

Perception (Jupiter?) is preferring to go with the flow, being flexible and responding to things as they come up.

Today, what's called the Big Five personality model is popular. In this assessment method, five factors, actually scales, are considered (these can be remembered with the acronym OCEAN or CANOE). The five factors are:

1. openness to experience (inventive/curious vs. consistent/cautious)

2. conscientiousness (efficient/organized vs. extravagant/careless)

3. extraversion (outgoing/energetic vs. solitary/reserved)

4. agreeableness (friendly/compassionate vs. challenging/callous)

5. neuroticism (sensitive/nervous vs. resilient/confident)

With both the Myers-Briggs and Big Five personality models, a lengthy psychological questionnaire or interview is required to obtain scores that determine the relative importance of these categories. The basis of the results is therefore self-referential and the questionnaire should ideally be taken only by people with a good understanding of themselves, something that is, unfortunately, not all that common. While the factors in these tests, determined by personal responses, are certainly important in understanding personality, they are limited and they don't seem to overlap that well with the measures used in a standard astrological chart analysis. What this means is that comparing schemes like these, invented by psychologists, to an astrological assessment is like comparing apples with oranges. Astrology has its own ways of organizing information about personality and can produce information quickly and without the use of questionnaires. As will be described below, I've developed an alternate model of basic personality traits that overlaps with Myers-Briggs and the Big Five in some ways, but it is based entirely on the analysis of elements, qualities and hemispheres that can be easily seen in an astrological chart.

Building an astrological personality profile

This following exercise is good for developing the skills needed for astrological chart interpretation. By simplifying the number of factors to work with, learning what each means may come more readily – more can be learned later. Going through the procedure multiple times will eventually produce memory imprints that may serve as a template for intuition and synthesis. While the series of tabulations outlined below are not perfect, they do pull in a number of chart components that are at the core of understanding how a chart works in the broadest sense. Once the basics of a chart are understood, details can then be added. In this way skills for chart interpretation can be established on a firm foundation.

The method described below uses an astrological chart set up to contain only the houses, Sun, Moon and planets. It is much easier to initially work with the basics so don't be concerned with asteroids, nodes or other points just yet. The first step is to get point scores for the Ascendant, Sun, Moon and planets. Begin with the base scores noted below and then modify them if they are emphasized by angularity, elevation or Ascendant rulership. The example chart will be used here, blank templates can be found on in the appendix section of this book.

Base scores

Sun, Moon, and Ascendant = 3 points each.
Inner planets (Mercury, Venus and Mars) = 2 points each.
Outer planets (Jupiter, Saturn, Uranus, Neptune, and Pluto) = 1 point each.

What Astrology is ...And How to Use it

Point scores (P-Score)

The base scores are listed in the table below. The following three conditions will add points to some of these and they are listed below the base scores. When these are added, the results obtained are the Point Scores which will be used later. Note that the Ascendant can't be modified by these three conditions and that abbreviations are used for the planets and signs in the tables below.

Angular planets (those located within roughly seven degrees of the Ascendant, MC, Descendant, and IC) receive an additional score of 3 points.

Most elevated planet (closest to the M.C) receives an additional 2 points. If two planets are equidistant from the MC give both 2 points.

Ascendant ruler (the planet that rules the sign the Ascendant) receives an additional 2 points. In the case of Scorpio, Aquarius and Pisces, use both traditional and modern rulers (Mars/Pluto, Saturn/Uranus, Jupiter/Neptune) adding 1 point each. In the example chart, the Sun and Moon are close to the angles and Neptune is the most elevated planet. Because Aquarius is rising, the rulership of the Ascendant will be split between Saturn and Uranus.

	Asc	Su	Mo	Me	Ve	Ma	Ju	Sa	Ur	Ne	Pl
Base score	3	3	3	2	2	2	1	1	1	1	1
Angular		3	3								
Elevated										2	
Asc ruler								1	1		
P-Score	3	6	6	2	2	2	1	2	2	3	1

Reading a Birth Chart

Zodiacal scores (Z-Score)

Now, having determined Point Scores for the Ascendant, Sun, Moon and planets, use these to get scores for zodiacal sign positions. For the Ascendant, Sun, Moon and planets, place each point score in the row of its zodiacal sign and then add the row to obtain the Zodiac Score.

Sign	Asc	Su	Mo	Me	Ve	Ma	Ju	Sa	Ur	Ne	Pl	Z-Score
Ar												0
Ta												0
Ge			6									6
Ca					2							2
Le		6	2					2				10
Vi						2					1	3
Li												0
Sc										3		3
Sa												0
Cp							2					2
Aq	3								1			4
Pi												0

Now, with both P-Scores and Z-Scores determined, we can begin to sort these out in a few ways. First, let's look at the scores for the elements – Fire, Earth, Air and Water. Using the **Z-Scores**, add them up for each element.

Fire signs = Aries, Leo, Sagittarius
Earth signs = Taurus, Virgo, Capricorn
Air signs = Gemini, Libra, Aquarius
Water signs = Cancer, Scorpio, Pisces

Fire	10
Earth	5
Air	10
Water	5

Here we see the same figures for Fire and Air signs, an indication that both are important and balanced in the example chart. Recalling that Fire and Air signs are both extraverted outward-facing signs and that Earth and Water signs which are introverted inward-facing, we could surmise that the person is probably extraverted.

Signs are also categorized by quality – Cardinal, Fixed, Mutable.

Cardinal signs = Aries, Cancer, Libra, Capricorn
Fixed signs = Taurus, Leo, Scorpio, Aquarius
Mutable signs = Gemini, Virgo, Sagittarius, Pisces

As was done for the elements, add up the **Z-Scores** for each of the qualities and place the sums in this box.

Cardinal	4
Fixed	17
Mutable	9

Here we see the figure for Fixed signs is much higher than the others. This could be taken to indicate a resistance to change and dedication – or stubbornness.

Hemispheres (H-Score)

How the planets are distributed around the chart can reveal much. There are two sets of hemispheres, above and below, and east and west. Simply count the planets that are above the horizon axis (Ascendant-Descendant) and those below. Each planet is worth only 1 point. Next, note how all the planets are distributed relative to the vertical axis (MC/IC) where east is on the left and west on the right of the chart. (Note: the Ascendant is not used as a score in these categories as it serves as an axis and the Sun, Moon and 8 planets always equals 10 points.)

Above	6		East	2
Below	4		West	8

Given that there are more planets above the horizon, the person is probably comfortable with public life, or at least has no serious problems navigating the outer, more objective world of social life. With more planets in the west, the person is strongly motivated by others and prefers partnership and cooperation over an individual path in life.

Ten personality traits

Using the P-Scores for angular planets, elevated or ruling planets, the Z-Scores for the elements and qualities, and the H-Scores for the hemispheres, along with the sign placements of specific planets, apply the results of the tabulations above to the personality inventory below. If one or more of the indications are met, then place the score for that indicator in the table that follows the list. This inventory measures personality extremes along a continuum much like a standard psychological personality profile. In most cases the scores will clearly point to a prominent personal quality. In some the scores will be even, an indication of a balance in that category.

1. *Self directed vs Other directed*. Is the person self-directed, independent and capable of taking action alone? Indications are:

   a. Fire-sign emphasis. _10_

   b. Majority of planets in the east. ____

   c. Sun, Mars, or Uranus angular. _6_

Or is the person other-directed, one who responds and is cooperative with others? Indications are:

   a. Majority of planets in the west. _8_

   b. Sun, Moon, or Ascendant in Libra or Pisces. ____

   c. Venus or Moon angular. ____

2. *Thinker vs Feeler*. Is the person predominantly left-brained, a thinker and analyzer of things who tends to rationalize and find logical solutions to problems? Indications are:

    a. Air-sign emphasis. __10__

    b. Mercury, Saturn, or Uranus angular. _____

    c. Moon or Ascendant in an Air sign. __6__

Or is the person predominantly right-brained, one who feels and knows intuitively what is going on and what to do? Indications are:

    a. Water-sign emphasis. _____

    b. Moon or Neptune angular. _____

    C. Ascendant ruler in a Water sign. _____

3. *Flexible vs Rigid*. Is the person flexible and adaptable? Do they strive to see multiple sides of an issue? Indications are:

    a. Mutable-sign emphasis. _____

    b. Mercury or Venus angular. _____

    c. Sun, Moon, or Ascendant in a mutable sign. _____

Or rigid and resistant to change? Indications are:

    a. Fixed-sign emphasis. __17__

    B. Sun, Saturn, or Uranus angular. __6__

    c. Sun, Moon, or Ascendant in Capricorn. _____

4. *Practical vs Idealistic*. Does the person tend to value what is practical and at hand? Indications are:

    a. Earth-sign emphasis. _____

    b. Sun, Moon, or Ascendant in an Earth sign. _____

    c. Saturn angular or most elevated. _____

Or does the person tend to look at life in terms of possibilities and ideals? Indications are:

    a. Air-sign or Fire-sign emphasis. _20_

    b. Sun, Moon, or Ascendant in an Air sign. _9_

    c. Neptune angular or most elevated. _3_

5. *Socially Active (extraverted) vs Private (introverted)*. Does the person prefer to be social and active in community matters? Indications are:

    a. Majority of planets above the horizon. _6_

    b. Air or Fire sign emphasis. _20_

    c. Sun, Mercury, Mars, or Jupiter angular. _6_

Or does the person prefer to be private and close to the home and family? Indications are:

    a. Majority of planets below the horizon. ____

    b. Water-sign emphasis. ____

    c. Sun, Moon or Ascendant in Cancer. ____

6. *Emotionally controlled vs Emotionally reactive*. Does the person control or repress emotions like excitement and anger? Indications are:

    a. Moon, Venus, or Ascendant in Air or Earth signs. _9_

    b. Saturn or Uranus angular or elevated. ____

    c. Fixed-sign emphasis. _10_

Or experience emotional urgencies that are expressed openly and directly? Indications are:

    a. Moon, Venus, or Ascendant in Fire signs. ____

    b. Moon, Venus or Neptune angular or elevated. _9_

    c. Water-sign emphasis. ____

7. *Leader vs Cooperater.* Is the person a natural leader, setting themselves apart from others and taking on leadership positions? Indications are:

   a. Sun or Mars angular. _6_

   b. Sun or Ascendant in Capricorn. ____

   c. Majority of planets in the east. _10_

Or is the person more comfortable working as a partner and adjusts to others personalities?

   a. Moon or Venus angular. _6_

   b. Sun or Ascendant in Earth or Water signs. ____

   c. Majority of planets in the west. _8_

8. *Organized vs Chaotic.* Does the person plan carefully, take responsibilities and display patience and concern for detail?

   a. Saturn angular or elevated. ____

   b. Fixed signs dominant. _10_

   c. Planets in Virgo. _3_

Or is the person more careless and unconcerned with specifics, not drawn to taking on responsibilities and generally letting things fall where they may?

   a. Neptune angular. ____

   b. Mutable signs dominant. ____

   c. Sun, Moon or Ascendant in Pisces. ____

9. *Extreme vs Moderating.* Is the person passionate about their causes to the point of being irrational?

   a. Mars, Uranus or Pluto angular or elevated. ____

   b. Mars or Moon in Water signs. ____

   c. Cardinal signs dominant. ____

Or do they weigh issues carefully and seek other to discuss such matters with?

    a. Venus or Saturn angular or elevated. ____

    b. Sun, Moon, Asc in Gemini, Virgo, Libra, Capricorn. _6_

    c. Air signs dominant. _10_

10. *Conservative vs Progressive.* Relative to their social world, does the person strive to preserve traditions or the status quo? Do they react strongly to people and ideas they are not familiar with?

    a. Earth and Water sign emphasis. ____

    b. Sun, Moon, Asc in Taurus, Cancer, Scorpio or Capricorn. ____

    c. Saturn or Mars angular or elevated. ____

Or do they see imperfections and strive to improve conditions in their social world? Are they tolerant of those who are different?

    a. Air and Fire sign emphasis. _20_

    b. Sun, Moon or Ascendant in Sagittarius or Aquarius. _3_

    c. Uranus or Neptune angular. ____

		(a)	(b)	(c)		(a)	(b)	(c)
1	Self-directed	10		6	Other-directed	8		
2	Thinker	10		6	Feeler			
3	Flexible				Rigid	17	6	
4	Practical				Idealistic	20	9	3
5	Extraverted	6	20	6	Introverted			
6	Controlled	9		10	Reactive		9	
7	Leader	6		10	Cooperates	6		8
8	Organized		10	3	Chaotic			
9	Extreme				Moderating		6	10
10	Conservative				Progressive		20	3

Applying these considerations to the example chart, we can learn that:

1. The person is probably self-directed because most of the planets are in fire signs and the Sun is angular.

2. The person is mentally active and an analyzer because the majority of planets and the Moon are in Air signs.

3. With the Fixed sign emphasis and the Sun angular, this person is rigid and resistant to change.

4. The person tends to be an idealist and see the potential in things due to the high score in Air signs, including the Ascendant and the Moon.

5. This person is socially active (extraverted) because Air and Fire signs are emphasized and the Sun is angular.

6. The person tends to be emotionally-controlled because the Moon and Ascendant are in Air signs and the chart has a Fixed-sign emphasis.

7. This person is more of a leader because the Sun is in Leo, a Fire sign, and near an angle. There is a tendency to compromise, however, due to a majority of planets in the west.

8. The person is organized and plans carefully because of a Fixed sign emphasis and planets in Virgo.

9. With planets in Air signs dominant and planets in Virgo and Capricorn the person is moderating and not an extremist.

10. The person is clearly a progressive thinker given the emphasis of Air signs, especially Aquarius.

General planetary distribution

The overall spread of the planets throughout the chart can be another clue into how a person operates, how broad or narrow their perspective is, how they handle conflicting views, and what special abilities they may have. The American astrologer Marc Edmund Jones proposed seven basic distribution patterns. These are as follows:

PATTERN	FORM	MEANING
Splash	Planets evenly scattered	Broad perspective, versatility
Bundle	Planets within 120°	Highly focused and specialized
Locomotive	Planets within 240°	Eccentric and dynamic, energized
Bowl	Planets within 180°	Self-contained (note hemisphere)
Bucket	Bowl + 1 planet outside	"Handle" indicates special abilities
See Saw	2 opposite clusters	Internalizes opposing views
Splay	3 separate clusters	Purposeful, strongly individualized

In the example chart we see a planetary distribution that approximates the locomotive pattern. Between Jupiter and Moon is about 120 degrees, and the rest of the planets are found within the remaining 240-degree range. This pattern suggests the person is driven, purposeful, energized and dynamic.

By following the above steps a good general sense of who a person is can be deduced. The description assembled should then serve as a foundation for understanding and an introduction to a chart reading, a basis for any additional insights that may be derived from a deeper chart analysis.

The chart we have just analyzed is that of President Barack Obama. What was found by considering just his Ascendant, Sun and Moon gave hints as to his personality. Adding the information found in tallying the elements and qualities enlarged this picture and said something about his fundamental orientations and behaviors – he scores high in fixed signs (solid, rigid) and Air signs (mental, communication). With many planets in the western hemisphere, rather than a pursuit of his own agenda (which would be the case if it were the eastern hemisphere emphasized), it is others, such as his wife, that play major roles. Others have had a powerful effect on him; during his presidency Congress continually blocked his agenda. However, he was successful when working with foreign leaders and did achieve some groundbreaking agreements. We see in the tabulation of points and positions a confirmation of these orientations and learn something about how he handles feelings and his social life. The elevation of Neptune highlights his great idealism and the locomotive distribution pattern of planets indicates that we are dealing here with a very strong and driven individual.

Of course, this simple analysis of his chart is only a start. A next step would be to take each planet by itself and interpret its nature in the context of the sign that it is in and its house position. For example, Venus in Cancer in the first house would suggest a prominent pleasing personality, but one that is traditional and conservative in certain ways. Aspects from other planets to Venus would add even more details. In this way more information can be added to the foundation established using the above techniques. Another approach would be to interpret each of the houses in order based on planets located in them or those linked to the house via rulership of the cusp. Developing a facility and style of chart reading takes time. Many years of experience interpreting astrological charts and comparing chart deductions to real people will develop the ability to mix and blend the planetary data of a chart necessary to produce useful information. But the above outline is a good way to start developing such skills.

Astrology and Self-Knowledge

Perhaps astrology's greatest value is found in self-knowledge. To be successful as individuals, we need to understand our own nature and how we interact with others. There are a number of routes to self-knowledge, including philosophy, psychology, religion, and just plain common sense. Astrology is an excellent path toward self-understanding and it can offer much more to the seeker than conventional routes, although it is generally not placed in that category due to prejudice and ignorance. In fact, astrology provides a sophisticated and coherent structure to the viewpoints that are provided by psychology, philosophy, religion, and most self-help books. Of the numerous models that attempt to explain the human situation, astrology is by far the most comprehensive.

Psychologists have observed that what we call personality is really a composite of several sub-personalities or themes. In astrology, these sub-personalities are focused in the parts of the birth chart, especially in the Ascendant, Sun and Moon. Over the past 100 years, psychologists have proposed a number of models that attempt to account for what might be called the plurality of the self. There is Freud's id, ego, and superego, and Jung's extrovert-introvert polarity and his four functions that now form the basis of the Myers-Briggs type inventory. Transactional analysis talks of the critical parent, the rebellious child, and the free child. None of these models can even begin to approach all of what astrology has to offer. The astrological chart is a stunning model of the self, its plurality, and its projections – and it's not just one psychologist's idea, it is a multi-millennial group project. I would argue that a complete understanding of just the Sun, Moon, Ascendant and their signs and aspects alone equals or surpasses anything that psychology has produced so far. Adding the other planets, aspects and the houses to this core opens the door to an even more expansive perspective.

The astrological chart shows the true nature of the self and the lines of least resistance in the development of personality. Genetics, family, society and culture have a powerful influence on individuals, shaping them in conformity with one tradition or another. Some people spend most of their lives fighting these forces, and they can become mentally and physically ill in doing so. Astrology offers a way of defining and acknowledging who we are, and of knowing who we are not. In this sense, astrology promotes free-will and intelligent choice.

Take as an example a man with the Sun in Pisces, who was born into a business-oriented family and, even with a string of successful business deals to his credit, felt somehow unfulfilled. Learning about the symbolism and needs of the sign Pisces from an astrologer led him to try his hand at art and eventually he became a successful painter. Without input from astrology, this might never have occurred to him because there had been no precedent for such activities in his family.

The Sun in the birth chart symbolizes the primary motivations in life, the activities and directions that give meaning to life. We should learn to follow our Sun-sign motivations, because they are ultimately central to our growth. A lifestyle built around our Sun-sign is empowering, vitalizing, and offers the best possibilities for overall integration of the self. While the Sun symbolizes who we really are, the Moon shows our interests, what we need to feed on. The Ascendant shows our social personality, the roles we play, how we come across to others, how we look, and how we mix with our friends, partners and family.

Self-knowledge is the first step toward wisdom. Knowing ourselves, we are masters of our destiny. Although a complete astrological perspective can only be provided through a reading of the birth chart in its entirety, there is a way to start a program of self-knowledge. Begin with a simple knowledge of Sun, Moon, and Ascendant sign which can provide a foundation for a better understanding of our true nature. Extend that with an understanding of Mercury, Venus and Mars which will provide even more personalized information about who we are and how we can improve.

Fate and Free-Will

Earlier in this guide the fate/free-will problem was discussed in the context of twins. The perspective of this author is that we are fated in several ways. First, we are a product of our genetics, about which we can do little. We are also restricted by our physical, emotional and mental predispositions which were formed during our childhood, characteristics we internalized from our parents and family. Only with tremendous effort and self-sacrifice can we overcome the constraints of genetics and family imprinting. These factors can be said to be our fate. In contrast, astrology tells us who we are and maps out our strengths and weaknesses. Contrary to the testimonies of the very successful, we may not be able to reach the top in any activity that we may choose – but we may be able to excel and find deep personal satisfaction and happiness in a field that is appropriate to our astrological chart.

Second, we are fated in the sense that our birth chart is ours for life and that when one of its cycles (planetary configurations) becomes active, we need to respond in some way. This is a kind of fate in the context of time. Our free-will lies in the quality of our responses to these needs. As we become more aware and conscious of who we are, we become capable of making more intelligent decisions and choices. Every choice we have to make is thus an opportunity to exercise our free-will. It is ignorance about who we are, irrational impulses, and unrealistic obligations to others that keeps us fated.

Relationships

Humans are social animals. In the final analysis, the quality of our lives is based on the quality of our relationships. We simply cannot ignore human relationships and any subject that provides reliable information about them should be considered valuable. Astrology offers several techniques by which relationships can be understood and evaluated. One technique, called synastry, involves comparing the planetary positions of one chart to those of another. Although the comparison of two birth charts can become quite technical and complex, there are a few general rules that anyone can apply when judging potential compatibility.

Rule #1. First, an understanding of how the zodiacal signs relate to each other is necessary. The listings below may be used for Sun-signs, but they are also applicable to other planets or points such as the Ascendant. See the table below for a summary of sign compatibility.

Ease of relationship: In general, a sign is compatible with other signs of the same element, that is they are in the same triplicity. For example, Aries is a Fire sign and will therefore be compatible with the other Fire signs, Leo and Sagittarius. There are common, natural and generally unconscious similarities between signs in the same triplicity that will support a relationship.

Fire signs: Aries, Leo, Sagittarius
Air signs: Gemini, Libra, Aquarius
Earth signs: Taurus, Virgo, Capricorn
Water signs: Cancer, Scorpio, Pisces

Another kind of compatibility is found between signs that share the same polarity. Fire and Air, both of positive or active polarity, have this connection. Likewise, Earth combines well with Water, both having negative or passive polarity.

Positive Polarity: Aries, Gemini, Leo, Libra, Sagittarius, Aquarius.
Negative Polarity: Taurus, Cancer, Virgo, Scorpio, Capricorn, Pisces.

Challenges to relationship: Compatibility between signs that are opposite each other can vary. In some cases relationships between people of opposite signs may become stressful because of differences. In other cases, they complement each other well, this depending on the level of communication between two people. Below is a listing of the opposite signs.

Aries - Libra	Cancer - Capricorn	Taurus - Scorpio
Leo - Aquarius	Gemini - Sagittarius	Virgo - Pisces

Signs that share the same quality may have more challenges in finding commonality. Recall there are three qualities: cardinal, fixed and mutable, each of which contains four signs. For any given sign, one of these is opposite, the other two are at right angles (the square aspect). Signs at right angles sometimes work at cross purposes and will require good communication and tolerance.

SIGN	TRIPLICITY	POLARITY	OPPOSITE	CROSS
Aries	Leo, Sagittarius	Gemini, Aquarius	Libra	Cancer, Capricorn
Taurus	Virgo, Capricorn	Cancer, Pisces	Scorpio	Leo, Aquarius
Gemini	Libra, Aquarius	Leo, Aries	Sagittarius	Virgo, Pisces
Cancer	Scorpio, Pisces	Virgo, Taurus	Capricorn	Libra, Aries
Leo	Sagittarius, Aries	Libra, Gemini	Aquarius	Scorpio, Taurus
Virgo	Capricorn, Taurus	Scorpio, Cancer	Pisces	Sagittarius, Gemini
Libra	Aquarius, Gemini	Sagittarius, Leo	Aries	Capricorn, Cancer
Scorpio	Pisces, Cancer	Capricorn, Virgo	Taurus	Aquarius, Leo
Sagittarius	Aries, Leo	Aquarius, Libra	Gemini	Pisces, Virgo
Capricorn	Taurus, Virgo	Pisces, Scorpio	Cancer	Aries, Libra
Aquarius	Gemini, Libra	Aries, Sagittarius	Leo	Taurus, Scorpio
Pisces	Cancer, Scorpio	Taurus, Capricorn	Virgo	Gemini, Sagittarius

Rule #2. Compare symbols which are similar. Examples: Sun to Sun, Moon to Moon, Ascendant to Ascendant, Venus to Venus, etc.

Compatibility of Sun-signs is important for long-term relationships. Because the Sun sign indicates the basic motivations and goals in life, incompatibility here may produce stress, avoidance, and the possible domination/submission of one individual to the other.

Moon-sign compatibility is important where family matters and living together is concerned. It indicates the general interests, emotions, moods, and eating and sleeping habits will not conflict seriously.

Ascendant compatibility is important where two people must make a good showing together in front of others. Ascendant compatibility also indicates that two people will appreciate the general appearance of each other.

Venus compatibility is important in intimate relationships because it symbolizes the way a person loves and what they value in love. People with their Venus positions in compatible signs will understand each other's loving style easily.

Rule #3. Note the relationship between the Sun of one person and the Moon of the other. Also note any interconnections between the Moon of one and the Ascendant and MC of the other. Relationships are likely to prosper where the Sun sign of one person relates favorably with the other person's Moon sign. This is also true when the Moon of one partner is in conjunction with the Ascendant, MC, Descendant, or IC of the other. These connections between two charts are often signs of family and domestic matters, suggestions that those domains will figure into the relationship.

Synastry, the Composite Chart, and the Relationship Chart

The judgment of the planetary contacts between two charts is called synastry. While the preceding section might serve as a foundation to this topic, the serious study of synastry can become quite complex and requires mastery of several astrological techniques. It is possible through synastry to judge a number of things about a relationship including major partnership issues, sexual attraction, communication potential, and relative dominance. For example, sexual attraction is shown when a person's Mars is connected by aspect to another person's Ascendant, Moon or Venus. People who have their Mercury in favorable aspect to another's Moon, Sun or Mercury will communicate easily. Those with squares between their Mercury and another's Ascendant, Sun, or Moon will need to work at communicating.

The *composite* chart is also used in evaluating a relationships; this is a chart that is derived by combining two natal charts. To create a composite chart, the zodiacal midpoints of each matched pair of planets and houses must be computed. For example, if one person has the Moon at 5 degrees of Aries and the other has the Moon at 5 degrees of Leo, then the composite Moon would be at 5 degrees of Gemini, half-way between the two. The composite chart shows how the relationship functions as an entity in itself and is often used in evaluating established relationships like marriages and business partnerships. Composite charts can also be constructed for three or more people and are useful in evaluating group dynamics.

The *relationship* chart is a chart calculated for the midpoint in time and space between two births. Here's an example. One person was born on December 21st, 1965 in New York City. Another was born on June 21st, 1966 in Los Angeles. The midpoint in time between their births was March 21st, 1966, and the midpoint in space was in Kansas. Their relationship chart would then be a chart calculated for March 21st, 1966 in Kansas. Like the composite chart, this chart is descriptive of how the two individuals blend.

9

Predicting with Transits

The astrological chart is a time-slice, a moment frozen in time. The positions of planets at that time might be compared to a printed circuit, a set of permanent connections that hold a fixed position. These positions will be sensitive points for an individual (or an event) throughout the course of life. As time passes and the planets move ahead in their orbits, they occupy or make aspects to these sensitive points in the birth chart. Transits are the connections that form between the present-day planetary positions and those that occurred at the time and place of birth. The transiting planet essentially activates a natal planet.

For example, suppose that the Sun's position at birth was 15 degrees of Aries. In November of 2020 Mars was at 15 degrees of Aries. This connection between the Sun at birth and Mars in 2020 constitutes what is called a transit, expressed in astrology as "transiting Mars conjunct the natal Sun." Because Mars is associated with activity, assertiveness, and friction, one could say that in November 2020, anyone born with the Sun near 15 degrees of Aries was likely to find their lives more active than normal and possibly even stressful. This effect would also be noticed, perhaps even more acutely, by those born with the Sun near 15 degrees Libra, which is opposite, or 15 degrees of Cancer or Capricorn, which are the squares.

The transiting planet brings its qualities to the natal planet that it contacts in the birth chart. Just being in the same or opposite sign as the Sun, Moon, or Ascendant is enough for the trend symbolized by the transiting planet to become readily apparent. This is particularly true of the transits made by the slower-moving planets. Even when a transiting planet enters the first degree of the natal Sun, Moon or Ascendant sign, or its opposite, an effect may be felt.

The mechanism for this (exactly how the transits are able to affect us) is unclear at present. It appears that transits activate or release the potentials of the natal chart in certain ways. They seem to trigger the "printed circuits" of our birth charts in a way that steers our experiences in a direction specified by the symbolism involved. The time lag between the transit and the experience can vary. Some people seem to respond immediately to a transit, others respond after a short delay. Responses also seem to be affected by the transiting planet – Mars effects are usually seen early, Saturn effects come later. It is possible that transits activate brain circuits that move us to register more vividly the things that are symbolized by the transiting and transited planets. In other words, transits create highlights in our consciousness that cause us to move towards or away from specific stimuli. Since an explanation for how astrology really works is years away, this is just an hypothesis.

Learning About Transits: An Exercise

Because we can calculate the positions of all the transiting planets well into the future, we can predict trends in a person's life experience - such information can help give structure to the otherwise seemingly arbitrary changes in their life. Below is a set of guidelines for working with a birth chart and the exact positions of the transiting planets. It is quite easy to learn this approach to understanding the future (as well as the past and present). Readers who have a facility for geometry will be able to do the exercise completely in their heads.

If you decide to become your own astrologer, keep two things in mind. First, a forecasting system based only on transits is limited and will not account for all the changes and developments that a person may experience. There are other, more complex systems that must be combined with transits in order to get a more complete picture. Second, it can take up to a year to begin to grasp the way life works when viewed from the astrological perspective. You may need to become a better observer of yourself and others and revise some of your assumptions about how things work. If you follow the rules, do the homework, and give some real thought to what you see, you will acquire a useful tool that will serve you well when you use it with understanding and restraint. The basic rules are as follows:

1. Have an accurate birth chart calculated. This can be accomplished online, from software, from a competent astrologer or your own calculations.

2. Buy an ephemeris (book of planetary tables) or find one online. This will allow you to determine the position (zodiacal longitude) of any planet on any day. Recommended: *The American Ephemeris* (midnight version).

3. Buy a book that delineates the various transits. Recommended: *Planets in Transit* by Robert Hand.

4. Construct a sensitive point list for your own birth chart, showing the degree and minute of every aspect to every point in the birth chart, organized in zodiacal order. With this list, you can easily determine transits to planetary positions in the natal chart. You may want to begin with only the five basic Ptolemaic aspects (the conjunction, sextile, square, trine, and opposition) and then later add others.

Here is an example of how to start a sensitive point list. Suppose that the natal Moon is located at 10 degrees and 30 minutes Virgo. Using just the Ptolemaic aspects, a total of eight points in the zodiac are calculated. There are then listed in zodiacal order. Transits to the Moon will then occur when planets are located at one of these points.

Conjunction at 10 degrees 30 minutes of Virgo (10♍30)
Opposition (180 degrees away) in Pisces (10♓30)
Square (90 degrees away) in Gemini and Sagittarius (10♊30 or 10♐30)
Trine (120 degrees away) in Taurus and Capricorn (10♉30 or 10♑30)

Predicting with Transits

Sextile (60 degrees away) Cancer and Scorpio (10♋30 or 10♏30)

Aspecting points to the Moon placed in zodiacal order:

10 ♉ 30 = trine
10 ♊ 30 = square
10 ♋ 30 = sextile
10 ♍ 30 = conjunction
10 ♏ 30 = sextile
10 ♐ 30 = square
10 ♑ 30 = trine
10 ♓ 30 = opposition

After you calculate all the aspect positions for all the natal planets, plus the Ascendant and MC, arrange them in the order of the zodiac signs, starting with Aries. Then, if you were to look in the ephemeris and find that Mars is passing through the sign of Cancer, you could turn to your section of Cancer listings and determine what connections transiting Mars would be making to your birth chart. You could also determine the days on which these transits would happen.

5. Do some basic personal research using this list of aspects. First, make a list of major events in your life and then correlate them with the positions of the transiting planets at those times. Second, determine when transiting planets were aspecting your birth chart, and then correlate this information with what was actually happening in your life at that time. Use an orb of one degree for the slower-moving outer planets. Only by working carefully with your own chart will you begin to understand clearly the kind of response you have to each planet. Don't be surprised if you seem to experience the effects of a transit a few days before or after it is exact. Everyone will respond somewhat differently to a given transit. Because there are other predictive techniques (progressions, directions, returns, etc.) besides transits in some cases no effects will be seen. A professional astrologer uses their experience

and takes this into account. You can become very competent at interpreting your own birth chart if you follow these suggestions.

6. In a calendar or datebook, write down the transits to your chart on the appropriate days. While the faster-moving planets may register trends and events on the day they make an exact aspect, give the slower-moving planets a week or two to make their presence felt. Do this for a month or two in advance. As time passes, make notes of what happened. Read about the transits as you live through them. Do not attempt to predict for yourself or to alter your plans radically until you have mastered these basics of calculation and observation. This exercise allows you to enter the world of astrological symbolism as it is unfolding.

The Transits of the Planets

As the planets move through their orbits, they make aspects to the degree-positions that they were in at birth. Each transiting planet has a general effect as described below. The specific effects of a given transit are shown by the natal planet it aspects, the nature of the aspect being made, the natal planet's house and sign position, and any other aspects that natal planet receives. Another variable to consider is that all transits will be technically exact at some point, but not all will produce effects right at that time. In general, the slower a planet moves, the more power it has in the birth chart. When planets are about to turn retrograde or direct, their motions are particularly slow and their effects become very strong. These nearly motionless points where the planets turn around are called stations. The effects of a transit of fast-moving Mercury will normally amount to very little, but when it stations it has the power of Jupiter or Saturn.

Sun: The Sun livens up whatever planet it is transiting, and it will emphasize the function of the transited planet for a day or two near the time the transit is exact. Often, authority and leadership issues are raised by the Sun's transit.

Moon: Lunar transits are quick, often lasting only a few hours. In some cases, clearly discernible events occur within just a few minutes of the Moon's exact aspect to a natal planet. Most Moon transits are subtle, but they do affect people on subconscious levels and will generally stimulate feelings, needs, or desires that lead them to change what they are doing at the time.

New and Full Moons: At the New Moon the Sun and the Moon occupy the same degree for about an hour. If this degree is the same as that of a natal planet, Ascendant, or MC, the New Moon is then a double transit and its effects can be quite noticeable. A New Moon exactly conjunct a point in the birth chart will activate that point strongly, forcing attention to the issues symbolized for several days. The same is true for the Full Moon, though in this case two opposite points become simultaneous transits. Eclipses are precisely focused New and Full Moons which pack even more power. Their effects can last for months.

Mercury: Mercury brings out the need to use our minds, to communicate and to negotiate the world around us. Mercury transits are quick, lasting only a day or two. When Mercury stations during its retrograde movement, however, its effects become far more powerful. Mercury transits affect communications and transportation. Calls, talks, messages, paperwork, writing, and information processing become emphasized and tend to require more attention. Also, transportation matters including driving, riding, walking, and mobility in general, become prominent themes or pressing issues.

Venus: Venus brings out the need to meet, join, harmonize with, and generally relate to others. Social interactions are increased or emphasized when this planet is transiting over important parts of a birth-chart. Venus transits coincide with meetings, gatherings, parties, consultations, and any partner-related events. People also feel a need to get emotionally involved with others when under a Venus transit and will make efforts to do so in one form or another. People with artistic, decorative or fashion interests will be active in these areas during a Venus transit. Although a typical Venus transit may last only a day or two, Venus in retrograde motion will emphasize the part of the birth chart it passes through for several months.

Mars: The need to move personal agendas forward and get thing done is stimulated under Mars transits. Common themes during a Mars transit are energetic activity, quick reactions, and conflicts. People experiencing a Mars transit will become busier, more energetic, more self-directed, more determined, and more assertive. They will be moved to take the initiative and not wait for others to do things first. Mars transits will coincide with construction projects, competitions, sports and athletic events. Mars transits can be challenging and some people will struggle with self-control issues. Impulsive actions and obliviousness to the existence of other people sometimes results in arguments, conflicts, and even accidents. Mars transits generally last for at least several days.

Jupiter: This planet brings increases and growth. Positively, a Jupiter transit stimulates confidence and optimism, bringing opportunities and abundance. Jupiter transits stimulate positive thinking on the "big-picture" level and can move people to do things based on what they believe to be right. Negatively, Jupiter transits coincide with excesses, too much of a good thing, and a tendency to blur the distinction between opinions and truth. Travel, learning, educational matters, philosophy, religion, and law may be a part of a Jupiter transit. Jupiter transits have an influence that generally lasts for a week or two, but in some cases for several months.

Saturn: Saturn transits bring problems, pressures, responsibilities, separations and awareness of limits. During Saturn transits, people generally find that they have less freedom and more responsibility. Authority figures or high standards will normally figure into the transit's influence in some way. Saturn transits don't allow for sloppiness or avoidance, they demand quality, practicality, and solidity. People who have a hard time accepting delays, obstacles, and reality may become frustrated and depressed under a long Saturn transit. Others, more in touch with consensus reality, will "chop wood and carry water" during the duration of the transit and emerge from it with something substantial accomplished. Nothing moves fast during Saturn transits; these are times when patience and endurance become valuable assets. Saturn transits are more acute around the time they are exact, but the trend can last for several months to a year.

Uranus: Disruptions and instability are the recognizable features of a Uranus transit. Uranus brings the need to change things and it is often the process of change itself that creates disturbances and instability. Typical Uranus transits bring completely new experiences, temporary and unique conditions that can't be repeated, unusual events, reforms, revolutions, and rebellions. People often respond to Uranus by first being rigid, then suddenly making a change that may surprise friends and family. A Uranus transit will bring out a person's need for freedom of self-expression. If this is not acceptable to the people around them, they will either rebel or make an attempt to change things. Uranus transits work suddenly and sometimes quite unexpectedly. The actual events of a transit may last for about a week, the repercussions may last for several months or longer.

Neptune: Positively, Neptune transits make people more sensitive to the arts and music, more compassionate and spiritual. Negatively, they will make people feel confused and overwhelmed by life, and the response may be escapist behaviors, denial, or isolation. Complex and unclear circumstances and misunderstandings are usually part of a Neptune transit. The challenge here is to move intuitively with the changes, to feel one's way through the complexities. Making sacrifices is part of the Neptunian theme. Neptune transits are good for volunteer work, spiritual matters, the arts, and the exploration of states of consciousness. The effects of major Neptune transits can be felt for months and even years.

Pluto: Pluto transits are very powerful and typically coincide with lifestyle changes and psychological crises. Pluto transits mark periods of time when people are forced into accepting transformations. They coincide with births, marriages, deaths, divorces, financial crises both positive and negative, psychological growth or challenges, medical issues, investigations, eliminations, and renewals. Pluto moves people to let go of situations in their life that are blocking personal evolution. On a deeper level Pluto challenges people to change their thinking and their internal programing (the psychological mechanism that attracts them to troublesome situations or people in the first place). Since Pluto moves so slowly, its transits last for a year, sometimes several years.

The Seven-Year Cycle

The so-called seven-year itch is a popular expression for a cycle that is shown astrologically by the transits of the planet Saturn. Saturn takes (on the average) 29.4 years to pass through all 12 signs of the zodiac. Dividing this period into quarters yields segments of 7.3 years each, when Saturn reaches the quarter, half, three-quarter, and completion points of its cycle.

Beginning at birth, there are successive periods of about seven years in a person's life, each one a stage of important adjustments to reality. At about 7 years of age, the first quarter of the transiting Saturn cycle, the first crisis of maturity occurs and self-awareness takes form. At about ages 14 or 15, the change from child to adult occurs. About 22 years of age brings adjustments to the demands of society. When Saturn completes its first cycle at about 29 years, people must come to terms with themselves and the society in which they live. This point in the cycle is called the Saturn return. It is almost always a time of important commitments, decisions, and the acceptance of responsibilities.

The next stages of the Saturn cycle occur at around the ages of 37, 44 (the peak of the mid-life crisis), and 52. Saturn again returns to its original position at about age 59. This second Saturn return is usually experienced more positively than the first, since most people are more settled and realistic at this point in life. The Saturn cycle marks the an important stage in personal and professional maturity, a need for completion, the acceptance of reality, the need for security, and changes in responsibility in any number of human activities. Crisis points can be observed in relationships or marriages at 7.3 years after the first meeting or the wedding. A store owner may need to make crucial business decisions 14.6 years after opening, and so forth.

The Graphic Ephemeris

The transits of the planets throughout the year can be shown visually on what is called a graphic ephemeris. These can be produced using some astrology software programs. On the graph below the vertical scale (y-axis) indicates the degrees from 0 to 90. The horizontal scale (x-axis) shows time, in this case three months of the year. On the graph, notice that the Sun is at 10 degrees on January 1 and travels to 40 degrees by February 1, its passage shown as a diagonal line across the graph. Notice that about a third of the way through January it intersects Mercury and then Saturn and Pluto just as they were crossing each other. The outer planets, like Saturn and Pluto, which move very slowly, are easy to spot on the graph because their lines change gradually. The inner planets are shown by lines that are much steeper. Mercury, for example, can easily travel the full 30 degrees of a sign in less than a month. Notice that in February Mercury stations and moves retrograde until March when it turns direct again.

You can track the transits against your own chart by adding horizontal lines across the graph at the degrees of the planets and points in your natal chart. For example, if you have the Sun at 15 degrees of Aries, you would draw a line through the 15 degree mark. By locating where the lines of the transiting planets cross the lines of your natal chart, you can determine when a transit will occur. Because the graph is only 90 degrees (the 12 signs are divided into quarters and collapsed onto each other), you will have to determine just what aspect is being made. Only the following aspects are possible using this graph: conjunction, square and opposition. A crossing of a planet line could be a conjunction, a square or opposition; only the name of the signs involved will tell you which one. Regardless of what aspect is being made, the important thing is that contacts between planets are clearly noted.

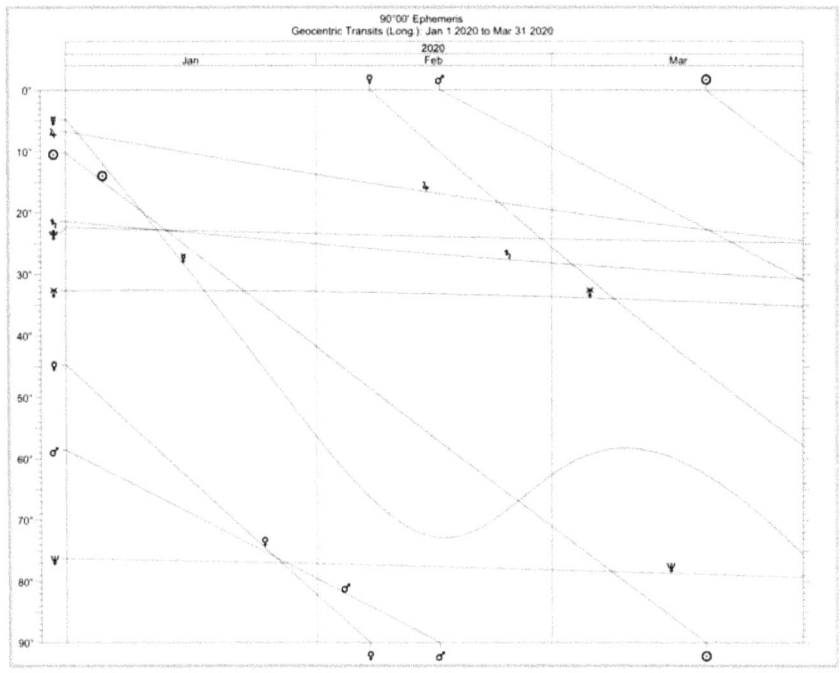

Figure 12. Graphic Ephemeris

Graphic ephemerides can be based on other segments of the zodiac. One format is 30 degrees which will show conjunctions, semi-sextiles, sextiles, squares, trines, quincunxes and oppositions. Another uses 45-degrees which includes conjunctions, squares, oppositions and the semisquare and sequisquadrate. In 45-degree graph, the vertical column goes from 0 degrees to 45 degrees. In terms of the zodiac it goes from 0 degrees of the Cardinal signs to 15 degrees of the Fixed signs, then from 15 degrees of the Fixed signs to 0 degrees of the Cardinal signs where it starts again. The 8 segments of the zodiac created in this way are then stacked and graphed. None of these formats are perfect so you will have to look at the signs involved in order to determine exactly which aspect is being formed.

Symbolic Substitution

Anyone who follows the transits to their natal chart for a few months will come to the conclusion that they work. It will also become obvious that no two transits involving the same planets will result in the same effect, yet whatever transpires is always within the limits of the symbolism involved. Mars transiting the natal Moon, for example, may at one time coincide with a conflict with a woman. At another time there might be a home repair with associated hammer-banging. At another time, there may be a stomach upset caused by too many red hot peppers. The Mars/Moon symbolism is consistent in all three events – Mars is anger, force, and irritation, while the Moon is female, home, and stomach. An astrologer friend of mine saw that he would be having a very strong Mars transit and thought it might be better to leave his city neighborhood where muggings were becoming common. He traveled to the mountains and camped out for a week in the wilderness to escape potential danger but instead had to fend off porcupines and raccoons that invaded his campsite each night. This suggests that at least the external effects of transits are relative to the environment one is in at the time. But how do we know which form a transit will take?

Most probably, transits activate forces deep within us that manifest in whatever symbolically-appropriate forms are immediately available. In the case of Mars transiting the Moon, some sense of urgency (Mars) is felt in the subconscious security system (Moon). When these forces rise to the surface of consciousness, they manifest with the appropriate symbols directing a person's feelings or urgings. The current environment apparently also shapes the affects of a transit – some things can only happen in certain places. Isn't it possible, then, to use free-will to choose what form the symbols might take? The astrological theory of Symbolic Substitution suggests exactly that. Because we can anticipate exactly when a transit will occur, we can steer ourselves toward more productive manifestations of the planetary energies by choosing our actions and our environment.

For example, if we know that Mars will be transiting the Moon, it is possible to deliberately create a Mars-Moon event. For instance, plan to do some-thing active or constructive with a woman, or perhaps paint the house red, or maybe set up a situation where one can vent anger in an appropriate manner. This is electional astrology at its finest – being creative with free-will, but staying within the context of the symbolism.

Other Astrological Predictive Techniques

Transits to the natal chart are only one of a number of methodologies that astrologers use to evaluate trends and make forecasts. Most ephemerides and astrological calendars will include listings of when the transiting planets make aspects to each other. These connections apply mostly to group behaviors and are reflected in the news, but they can also be used personally. The planet that rules the Ascendant in a chart carries with it a strong connection to that chart and its aspects to other planets will be reflected in the person's life. For example, a person with Libra rising will be affected by transiting Venus' alignments with other planets. When Venus is conjunct, square or opposition Saturn, in any sign, the Libra rising person will experience delays, constraints and separations. When Venus aspects Jupiter, the person will more than likely have a good day. The same logic applies to the other Ascendants and their ruling planets.

One of the oldest predictive techniques is called Primary Directions, in which angles of the birth chart are "directed" to the planets in the birth chart at a specific rate. In essence, this technique takes the birth chart and moves it ahead, correlating one degree of motion at the MC to one year of life. It is the rotation of the Earth after the birth moment that is measured when using directions. If a chart has the MC at 10 degrees of Libra, and Saturn is located at 15 degrees of Libra, then the MC would be directed to Saturn at age 5 – and a corresponding trend would occur.

Another technique is Secondary Progressions. This popular predictive system uses the correlation of a day-for-a-year to determine how a person might experience any given year. If the person is 45 years old, the planetary positions on the 45th day after birth are examined. By working proportionally (24 hours = 1 year, 2 hours = 1 month) very exact forecasts can be made. Solar Arc directions is a technique which involves finding the distance in degrees between the progressed Sun (one day-for-a-year) and the natal Sun, and then applying this distance to the other planets. This technique, popularized by the Hamburg School of Astrology (Uranian Astrology) could be considered a form of secondary progressions.

The MC in Primary Directions moves ahead by roughly one degree per year, and so does the progressed Sun. A very simple way of seeing patterns in the future is to simply take the number of degrees between two points and translate them into years. While this is an approximation, it requires no calculations other than subtraction. If a chart shows several pairs of planets that are the same number of degrees apart, this would be a clue that the corresponding age would be important. For example, Barack Obama was 45.5 years old when he announced his campaign for the presidency and 47.5 years old when he assumed office. Looking at his chart in Chapter 9, if Mars is moved ahead in the zodiac by 46 degrees it will come to Neptune. This is interesting as Mars is the ruler of his MC (in Scorpio) that signifies profession and public life and Neptune is the most elevated planet. Also, if Venus is moved ahead in the zodiac it will reach the Descendant (the point opposite the Ascendant) in 46 degrees. Since the Descendant is one of the four angles, it is a very powerful point and suggests an significant increase in meetings and social life in general. It would seem, then, that 46 years of age would mark an important development in his life.

Another technique, Solar Returns, is the construction of charts cast for the exact moment in any year that the Sun returns to its exact birth position. These charts offer information about the year ahead. The same technique is used with the Moon to calculate Lunar Returns, charts that are read for the month ahead. Astrologers vary in their methodologies. Some favor solar and lunar returns, other don't use them at all. There is no single way to do astrological forecasting.

10

Following the planets

Learning about and coming to understand your natal chart and those of people you know is probably the best way to learn astrology. As the planets move along their orbits and make aspects to natal points one can get a good sense of personal rhythms, reactions and behaviors. A transiting planet activates a natal planet and correlates with personal trends. The same is true of other more complex predictive techniques. All of this is self-centric, an understanding of how the solar system impacts a single life. Most of natal astrology is concerned with the experiences and concerns of the self.

There are social dimensions that play a role in natal astrology, however. One is in the form of relationship astrology such as synastry and composite charts. Another is in the phenomena of projection, where points in a natal chart actually describe qualities of personality and events in the lives of close others. For example, the Moon and Venus in a male's chart are descriptive of the women in their life – mother, wife, daughters. Likewise, the Sun and Mars in a female's chart describes to some extent father, husband and sons. This projection phenomenon, known well in psychology, reveals how history and society has shaped gender issues and is a fascinating and even controversial topic in itself. But all of the above are astrological realities that stem from the natal chart.

A completely different perspective lies outside of the self. In the world at large are other people, groups, communities, culture, politics and other large-scale social environments. There is also the natural environment – weather and climate. These external worlds respond to the astrological effects of the planets as they relate to themselves, not just natal charts. As we live our lives the phases of the Moon change, Mercury goes retrograde and planets form conjunctions and other alignments. This is the external astrological "weather" that needs to be considered if the self is to better understand the world and navigate it more efficiently. The most immediate way of engaging in this external world is to practice some of the techniques of electional astrology.

Choosing the Best Time to Take Action

Electional astrology seeks out the best times to commence an action. It is a traditional branch of the subject that was practiced in ancient times and applied to activities like the launching of a ship, the starting of a war or a coronation. By observing the astrological conditions at the start of a project or event, astrologers over many centuries learned what worked best and then applied this knowledge to future conditions. In a wide sense, electional astrology is an act of free-will, though the Church didn't see it that way and it has been described as a kind of ritual magic. While professional astrologers study future planetary positions in great detail and use this knowledge to select a time to act, a lot can be accomplished by following the simple concepts described below.

The Phases of the Moon

Many calendars show the four main phases (aspects) of the Moon each month, a tradition that dates back to the times when the livelihoods of farmers and seafarers depended on such information. The diagram below shoes the four phases of the Moon: (1) new Moon (Moon conjunct Sun), (2) first quarter (Moon square Sun), (3) full Moon (Moon opposite Sun), and (4) third quarter (Moon square Sun). After the third quarter the Moon will be on its way back toward the new Moon phase. This is a synodic cycle, a cycle of two bodies from Earth's perspective, in this case the Sun and Moon.

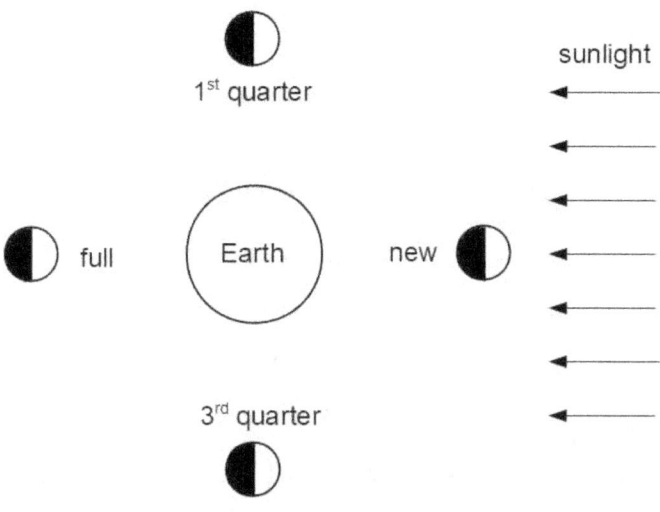

Figure 13. Lunar Phases

For centuries, people have planned their activities around this Sun-Moon cycle. Connections have been made between it and the tides, when to plant, how much light would be available during the night, what the weather might be like and when an action taken would get good results. Much of this knowledge has been lost during the past few centuries as our civilization has moved farther away from an immediate connection with nature. We still know a few things about the Moon, however. We know that the highest tides occur at full and new Moon, and that people's behaviors may intensify around the Full Moon. There are often heavy rains, and the stock market fluctuates noticeably, about three to five days after New and Full Moons. The following are a few traditional general rules about the Moon that have proven their worth over time.

1. Start important new activities (such as opening a business, planting a garden, getting married, building a house, etc.) between the New Moon and the Full Moon (the first half of the cycle). The closer to the Full Moon, the more rapidly the activity will proceed. Move to finish up incomplete projects,

or start secret or hidden projects, between the Full and New Moon (the second half of the cycle).

2. Do not start important activities on the exact day of the New or Full Moon, or within a day of the quarter Moon. Activities started at the quarter are likely to prove more difficult or develop major problems later.

3. Make important decisions at the Full Moon. The Full Moon is a time for deep understanding, a time for insight, clarification, objectivity and a time for making choices in regard to relationships.

Using Lunar Aspects

The Moon takes just over two days to travel (transit) through a sign. During this time it forms aspects with the other planets, some favorable, some stressful. There are many astrological calendars and ephemerides which list these lunar aspects, some even giving the exact time of day that each aspect occurs and also the time that the Moon is "void-of-course" (see below).

In general, when choosing a date to do something like traveling or opening a business, it is better to choose a day when the Moon forms positive aspects (trines and sextiles) to the other planets. The one day each month when the Moon is conjunct Jupiter is usually a good day to start a project that you want to grow. Conversely, it may be best to avoid beginning important projects on days when the Moon forms many adverse aspects (squares and oppositions) with the other planets, particularly with Saturn.

The Void-of-Course Moon

After the Moon has completed making all its aspects with the other planets, it must finish its transit through the sign that it is in. This period of time, which begins when the last lunar aspect occurs and finishes when the Moon enters the next sign, is the time when the Moon is *void-of-course*. This period can last anywhere from a few minutes to a day or more, depending on where the other planets happen to be located. Traditionally, only the Ptolemaic aspects (the conjunction, sextile, square, trine, and opposition) are used in determining whether or not the Moon is void-of-course.

When the Moon is void-of-course it is best not to begin new projects or take unnecessary risks. More often than not, projects initiated under a void-of-course Moon will not produce hoped for results and things may go nowhere, be disappointing or end up requiring major adjustments and refinishing later. The time that the Moon is void-of-course is not a time for action, but rather for quiet and meditation. It is also good for catching up on unfinished business, reviewing, re-arranging things, and for simply letting things happen. Listings of when the Moon is void-of-course can be found online, in ephemerides and in many astrological calendars.

The Angularity of Jupiter, Sun and Venus

As we know, planets which are rising, setting, culminating, and anti-culminating (at lower culmination) are more powerful than when they are in other positions. In the same way, events which are started when a planet occupies one of these powerful positions tend to be strongly influenced by that planet. It is best to start projects or take risks when Jupiter, the Sun, or Venus (the traditionally beneficial planets) are near the Ascendant, MC, Descendant, or IC Conversely, one would not want to take risks when Saturn is angular. But if you wanted to do something formal, or something that was to endure, then Saturn would be an appropriate significator. As a general rule, determine the planet that best signifies what you want to do, then do it when that planet is angular and therefore at an energy peak in its daily (diurnal) cycle. There are four times each day when a planet is near an angle. With an understanding of the astrological chart, as outlined in earlier chapters, these periods can be found using chart-calculating apps for phones, certain websites, or with astrological software.

Mercury Retrograde

All the planets, with the exception of the Sun and Moon, will move in a reverse direction at times, called retrogradation. The planets beyond Earth's orbit, Mars through Pluto, will be in retrograde motion when they are roughly opposite the Sun – as seen from Earth. The two inner planets, Venus and Mercury, will retrograde when they are nearest Earth. The effects of retrograde planets are subtle in most cases. However, there is a planetary phenomenon that occurs three times per year that is very obvious to anyone who cares to pay attention to it. These are the periods when Mercury is retrograde. Paying attention to when Mercury is retrograde could save time and trouble, and make life easier and more comprehensible for many people. As Mercury orbits the Sun, it never actually goes backward, but it appears to do so from our vantage point on Earth. The diagram below shows how the changing perspective from Earth (outer orbit) to Mercury (inner orbit) can produce the phenomenon of retrogradation. As seen from the Earth, there is the following sequence of events:

1. Mercury speeds through four consecutive signs of the zodiac. Faster than any planet, its speed is exceeded only by that of the Moon.

2. Mercury then slows down and stops and begins to move in reverse. This is called Mercury's first station. Where this turning point occurs with respect to your birth-chart is very important for you.

3. For about three weeks, Mercury appears to move in a reverse direction, then slows down and stops for a second time. This is its retrograde movement and its second station. Again, where this station occurs in your chart is important.

4. Once more moving in its natural, "forward" direction, Mercury gradually gains speed. About six weeks after step #2 began, Mercury passes the point where it made its first station. This is sometimes referred to as Mercury

passing out of its shadow. The sequence of events is now complete, and Mercury moves ahead at top speed again for the next three months.

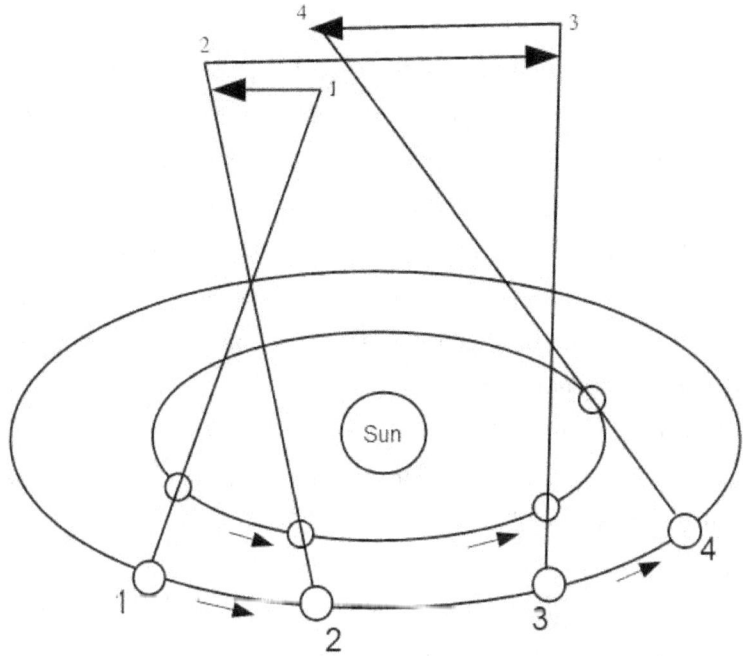

Figure 14. Mercury Retrograde

The part of your birth chart where Mercury makes its retrograde loop becomes activated in several ways. First, there is an emphasis on matters signified by the house in which Mercury goes retrograde. For example, Mercury retrograde in your seventh house would turn up the volume on relationship matters, particularly partnerships such as marriage. Second, if you were to initiate new, untried activities at this time, matters associated with this house would begin to become more complex and difficult to manage. For example, if you got married (for the first time) while Mercury was retrograding in your seventh house, you might have some serious problems related to communications with this marriage. But Mercury retrograde in the seventh house could indicate a favorable time to re-marry.

This is the secret of using Mercury retrograde to your advantage: While it's retrograde, do things you've already done before. The matters emphasized by the Mercury retrograde begin to return to normal around the time that Mercury passes its first station.

The sign in which Mercury retrogrades can provide useful information. Mercury retrograde in (or opposite) your Sun sign often indicates problems like paperwork overload, transportation complications, delays, and a general lack of progress – but it could also be a time when you catch up with unfinished business. On a worldly level, the stations of Mercury almost always coincide with major news events, often those involving transportation (airlines, traffic), communications (release of documents, public information) and weather events, most often high winds.

Those born with the Sun in Gemini or Virgo seem to be affected the most during the times when Mercury is retrograde, since both signs are said to be ruled by Mercury. This is also true of those born with Gemini or Virgo Ascendants. Astrologers have noticed that an unusual number of people born under these signs experience stress on the very days that Mercury makes a station. Most frequently, problems have to do with transportation, information, communication and perception. It is also true that those houses in a birth chart with Gemini and Virgo on the cusps are affected by this erratic planet. In general, and more so for those with Gemini, Virgo or Mercury prominent in their chart, it pays to be careful and patient when buying anything new by mail-order when Mercury is retrograde as items may be out of stock or not reach their destinations in a timely way. On the other hand, during Mercury retrograde it would be appropriate to purchase items that either had been bought before or complete an earlier purchase that requires renewal. These situations are more likely to proceed without problems.

Using mutual aspects

Ephemerides and astrological calendars often contain what's called an aspectarian, a listing of the aspects between the Sun, Moon and planets on a daily basis. Each day the fast moving Moon makes aspects with the other planets – until there are no more aspects to be made in that sign and it begins its void-of-course period. These lunar aspects operate on a short time scale, perhaps within a range of an hour or two. Meanwhile, other aspects between the Sun and planets form, these lasting for more than a few hours and often overlapping with other aspects. These connections between the Sun, Moon and planets are sometimes called the mutual aspects. They are events that pertain to general conditions, not a single natal chart.

Mutual aspects will have noticeable effects when they are exact, but certain conditions must be met. The first is a group must be present, the larger the group the stronger and more obvious the effect. For example, conflicts would likely arise at a party attended by more than 30 people held at a time when the Mars was making an exact square to Saturn, and the Moon was simultaneously making an opposition to Mars and a square to Saturn. If only two people were present, the effects would not be so obvious. These kinds of effects can also be seen by watching the news on a daily basis. Public meetings and governmental activities may run into problems, be frustrating or even fail when mutual aspects are challenging. They may be successful, however, when the aspects are more positive. On the personal level, the effects may be subtle, or non-existent, but looking at the mutual aspects before scheduling a group event is often a good idea. Note that specific times are usually given for each aspect, though be sure these times are for your time zone or they will need to be converted.

The second thing to keep in mind about mutual aspects is that some of them may be more personal than others. As was mentioned in the previous chapter, the planet that rules the sign on the Ascendant in the natal chart of a person is the one to watch. As it makes aspects with the other planets, personal effects may be apparent. For example, a person with Gemini rising will have Mercury as their Ascendant ruler. If, on a certain day, Mercury is square Saturn, that day may bring some constraints and delays. If Mercury was trine Jupiter, then personal matters would likely flow more smoothly. Aspectarians usually give the precise times that aspects become exact and these should be used when making any plans.

One other way to use the mutual aspects is to note when aspects form that replicate those in the natal chart. If a person was born with Mars opposite Venus, then when Mars and Venus move opposite each other in the sky, that person would experience the social friction and emotional charge that is characteristic of that aspect. They may also feel Mars-Venus energy when these planets make other aspects with each other as well. In this way, and also by using the Ascendant ruler, the mutual aspects found in an aspectarian can be used for personal matters.

The aspects of the major planets: mundane astrology

The outer planets, as they move in their orbits, align with each other over longer intervals of time. The correlations between the aspects of the outer planets and social trends, and even history, has been a topic in astrology since ancient times. It is today called mundane astrology. The two largest planets, Jupiter and Saturn have orbits around the Sun of about 12 and 29.5 years, respectively. They meet up with each other forming a conjunction every 20 years and it is thought that these great meetings mark important shifts in society and culture. Where these conjunctions form follows a pattern: each conjunction occurs about a trine earlier in the zodiac. The movement backwards of the conjunctions is not an exact trine and after roughly a century and a half the series of conjunctions will shift into another triplicity. This can be seen in the table below that shows the signs where Jupiter-Saturn conjunctions will occur from 1940-2100. The conjunctions took place

Following the planets

in the Earth signs beginning in 1802 and began to shift to the Air signs in 1980. The shift to the Water signs begins with the 2159 conjunction.

	1940	1961	1980	2000	2020	2040	2060	2080	2100
Ar									
Ta	x			x					
Ge							x		
Ca									
Le									
Vi									
Li			x			x			x
Sc									
Sa									
Cp		x							
Aq					x			x	
Pi									

What these Jupiter-Saturn conjunctions mean needs to be understood from a broad perspective, one of history. Mundane astrologers see them as indicators of the beginning of a 20-year socio-political cycle that ushers in a time of important and generally positive developments in financial and economic matters. Typically, there is change in governance, often a return to more traditional ways of handling problems and making decisions. New and different leaders are sworn in and policies are changed from those in place before the conjunction. In the USA, this usually indicates a change in political party leadership. In between the conjunctions Jupiter and Saturn will form other aspects, the squares the oppositions will often mark challenging times in financial markets and in politics. How things will go during these periods depends on the signs they are in and the positions of other planets as well.

Aspects between Saturn and Uranus often mark times of disruption and forced changes. The cycle of Saturn is 29.5 years and that of Uranus 84 years. Like the cycle of the phases of the Moon, their conjunction, squares and oppositions mark shifts and changes. With Saturn being the planet of norms, and Uranus being the planet of change and reform, and also technology, their aspects mark times of strong conflict between the old and new. The turbulence of the mid 1960s was correlated with the opposition of these two planets, as did the election of Barack Obama in 2008. The conjunction in 1988 led to the breakup of the Soviet Union and the fall of the Berlin Wall and the square in 1999 was marked by impeachment of the US president which disrupted politics.

1965	1975	1988	1999	2008	2021	2032	2043	2056
opp	squ	con	squ	opp	squ	con	squ	opp

The Uranus-Pluto cycle is one that appears to correlate with more serious cultural upheavals. With this combination revolutionary Uranus, which denotes individual rights, is ramped up by Pluto which is associated with power plays, rebellions and passionate, irrational popular movements that may reach a breaking point leading to wars. The length of the full cycle from conjunction to conjunction varies considerably due to Pluto's very elliptical orbit, but on average is about 127.5 years. Because these two planets move so slowly, the dates in the table below should be seen as the middle of a multi-year period, at least 3 years before and after the date. The cultural disruptions that occur during Uranus-Pluto aspects may percolate for years, erupting into major changes, sometimes violent, a decade later. For example, the conjunction of Uranus and Pluto in 1850 was followed by a decade political turbulence during which the USA became polarized over the issue of slavery in new states. This led to the Civil War. The next conjunction, in the mid 1960s, is associated with youth rebellion, social unrest and the beginnings of a number of progressive movements.

1793	1820	1850	1877	1901	1932	1966	2013	2047	2073
opp	squ	con	squ	opp	squ	con	squ	opp	squ

These three planetary pairs are by no means the final work on global trends. Other combinations involving Jupiter occur over shorter periods of time while Neptune-Pluto conjunctions occur only every 248 years. The three combinations given above have a reputation for change and one can learn much about mundane astrology by following them as the occur. Planetary combinations are never the same. They occur in different signs and often overlap each other making interpretation more complex. But they locate in time the relentless changes and evolution of terrestrial life.

Appendix A

The Astrological Reading

Having your birth chart read by a competent and experienced astrologer can be a powerful experience. It can help to give your life more structure by putting things into perspective, and it can suggest possible strategies for handling challenges. It may actually change your life. Astrology is a wonderful tool in the quest for self-knowledge, the foundation of all psychological and spiritual work. An astrological reading is like referring to a road map – and maps are a great help when you need to be better organized or make choices about which route to take. They are especially valuable on those rare occasions when you are actually lost! But keep in mind that maps are kept most of the time in the glove compartment, not thrown across the windshield where they obscure your vision. Likewise, too much astrology can be worse than too little.

Before seeking out an astrologer and making an appointment, be sure that you know the date, place, and exact time of your birth. A birth time error of only four minutes can make a substantial difference, especially in forecasting. If you don't have a birth certificate with the time of your birth and your relatives don't remember, you may be able to check with your local council or government authority, or the hospital where you were born. Online digitised resources are also available depending on your country.

If your time of birth is completely unknown, you have two options. You could settle for what is called a solar chart reading. Here, the astrologer calculates a chart for sunrise, or possibly noon, on the day you were born and attempts to read it as if it were your birth chart. In many cases, the results of this approach are reasonably accurate and helpful. Your other option is to have an astrologer determine your time of birth through a process called rectification. Using a list of dates of major events in your life, the astrologer will attempt to adjust the chart to fit the events. Rectification is extremely complex, time-consuming and costly. Expect to pay far more for this service than for a reading.

Now, hopefully in possession of accurate birth data, you must find an astrologer to do a personal reading for you. The internet is full of astrologers competing with each other for your attention. Who to make an appointment with can be overwhelming. Having a successful website or high fees are not necessarily indications of a good astrologer. Very well known astrologers may have very high fees and be booked a year or more in advance. You may want to seek out astrologers who have passed certification exams. Astrological organizations and certifying boards will give references if you ask them. If you have heard of an astrologer that has a good reputation do some research before you make a commitment. Do you feel more comfortable meeting with an astrologer in person or would you prefer a phone, Skype or Zoom consultation?

One way of deciding on an astrologer is to call and talk to them. You can often learn much in just a few moments of interaction. Be sure to assess his or her qualifications. How long has this astrologer been practicing? Are they a member of any astrological organizations? Have they taken any certification tests? Do they have a college degree? Any graduate degrees? Have they published anything? Do they teach classes? Does they have references? What is their philosophy of astrology? Keep in mind that many astrologers today are hobbyists, i.e., they practice astrology on the side. Some part-time practitioners are highly qualified and you may find their fees on the low side. As was mentioned in Chapter 2, certification tests are available to astrologers but, as with doctors, this is not a 100% guarantee of competency. When talking to an astrologer, don't forget to ask about their fees, the length of their readings, and when they take appointments.

The Astrological Reading

Having selected an astrologer and made an appointment, you may want to prepare yourself by reviewing some of the basic astrological concepts in this book. Making a list of the questions you have about yourself, your past and your future would also be helpful. Be sure that your reading is recorded, either by the astrologer or yourself, so that you may review it later. Often, so much is said during a reading that it takes several playbacks to assimilate the material.

Your astrologer will prepare for the reading by calculating your birth-chart. Today, most astrologers use computer software for this time-consuming job. Most astrologers will begin their reading of your chart with a discussion of your personality and life potentials. Using the positions of the planets in signs and houses, they will ascertain your life pattern from the symbols. Be patient, it may take a while for them to put it all together, but that's because each person is uniquely complex. (Compare this to the number of sessions it takes the typical psychotherapist to understand a person this thoroughly.) There is no single, universally approved format for reading charts. Some astrologers may wish to spend an entire session on just the birth chart alone and request that you schedule another session for predictive work. Others may combine both subjects in one reading. You will need to ask the astrologer ahead of time how they prefer to work.

Feel free to ask questions during the reading, and provide what may be relevant information. Without your input and feedback, the astrologer may not be able to locate which of several possibilities within a general category is the right one for you. This is the same technique as a doctor uses; knowing that you hurt, the doctor asks you exactly where it hurts and what kind of pain it is. Interactive dialogue between astrologer and client can be very productive, but let the astrologer do most of the talking.

Ask your astrologer about any other services they offer. Besides personality readings and forecasting, many astrologers today will analyze all types of relationships, including marriage, business partnerships, and parent/child relations. By comparing two birth charts, and also deriving a composite or relationship chart for the two, much can be learned about the potential of a relationship even before it has begun!

Your location on Earth can make a difference in your life. Some astrologers will be able to assess your potential in other places using the techniques of locational astrology. Ask if your astrologer is certified in this field or has worked with it extensively. Horary astrology, the art of reading a chart cast for the time a critical question was asked, and electional astrology, the choice of a best time to do some-thing, are specialty areas that your astrologer (or another) may be experienced in.

Each astrologer has their own orientation and way of working. Although most astrologers in the West practice tropical astrology, but some are knowledgeable of other traditions, such as Vedic (Hindu) astrology, and they may combine both systems. When it comes to forecasting, a number of techniques are available: the most often used are transits (the positions of the current planets compared to the birth chart) and progressions (a symbolic day-for-a-year method of timing life's events). Other forecasting techniques are solar and lunar returns, solar arc directions, and primary directions. In the hands of an expert, any of these techniques will work well.

Astrologers, like all counselors or consultants, differ philosophically. Some are psychologically oriented while others emphasize the spiritual side of life's events. Some are idealistic while others are pragmatic. Some are more fatalistic while others are more concerned with correct timing and making life run more efficiently. In the final analysis, there are as many kinds of astrologers as there are doctors or therapists. You'll have to determine which one is best for you.

Appendix B

Astrology software

Since the late 1970s it has been possible to work with astrology on a personal computer. For the first time in history, the laborious work of the calculations necessary to make astrological charts, transits, and progressions was no longer a major block to learning astrology. In many respects, the computer has made astrology more democratic and beyond the domain of the purely mathematically minded. Since about 2000 this labor-saving change also has a place online where a number of websites offer free calculations and others offer much more with a subscription.

Astrology software was among the earliest commercial software made, and it has revolutionized this subject in ways that were previously unimaginable. It seems that the computer has done for astrology what electricity did for the guitar – given it more power and brought it to a much wider audience. Since the introduction of personal computers the evolution of computer hardware, software, and peripherals has been remarkably rapid and shows no signs of slowing down. This marriage between astrology and the personal computer has created a number of interesting possibilities. People who have access to astrological software, on their personal device or online, can explore many facets of astrology with great ease. Much like a carpenter's toolbox, a good astrological program can provide many tools that are specific to the task needed to be done. Before computers, many of these astrological tools were inaccessible.

Some astrology computer programs are aimed at the professional practitioner who may use high-powered techniques and methods. Other types of software can be used by anyone to earn money by producing printed astrological reports. Some software allows users with astrological knowledge to take raw data from astrology programs and add interpretations of their own. This lets the user sell their own personally customized reports. Some software is aimed solely at the non-astrologer. This type of software lets the user create personal astrological reports that are built from previously prepared text blocks written by an astrologer. Software from all of these categories can be found online.

Today's astrological software can be divided into several basic categories. Your choice of software depends on your intentions, though you may have several interests that can be accommodated by one large program. There are a number of companies that produce astrological software and you can order from them directly. You can also find these software packages for sale on Amazon and other large distributors. Apart from the individual differences between the various software publishers, most astrological software on the market today falls within one of the following categories.

Low-End Introductory Software
These programs, many of which can be found online and used for free, are excellent for beginners and for those who simply want to calculate a chart or read interpretive text from the screen. Typically, these programs do not print any charts or text, though you can usually print what is on the screen by using certain keys on your keyboard. They are designed for browsing through a chart, looking at aspects or perhaps reading paragraphs that describe some of the chart's main features. One thing that should be stressed about these programs is that their calculations are usually very precise and you can count on the charts they produce to be accurate.

High-End Delineation Packages – Report Writers
These programs are highly specialized and offer quality astrological delineations that can be saved as an ebook, pdf or printed and bound into reports. Most individuals who purchase this type of software do so because they want to sell astrological reports online, and some have earned

considerable amounts doing so. In some cases the software producers offer valuable suggestions, even graphics, to help end-users get started in business. Report-writing programs are available for all major types of astrological delineation. Most popular are those that generate and print delineations of the natal chart. Many of these print out the astrological chart itself first and then sort out the relative weights of factors such as the elements, qualities and planetary distributions (much like what is described in Chapter 9). Then the programs delineate the chart planet-by-planet, house by house. Ordered online, the output can be purchased as a pdf or ebook. Some offer hard copies. By attaching a nicely designed front and back cover, and using a simple binding, the user of such a program can produce an attractive and helpful product, or gift, to interested friends and family.

Other report writers are available for relationships, including both synastry and the composite chart, progressions, transits, solar and lunar returns.[15] You can buy one of these and then add others as needed. For many, the reports generated by these programs are an excellent way to learn astrology and to follow the constantly changing trends in one's life. Prices vary widely depending on the complexity of the program and the amount of text that is produced. Some programs are designed to be compatible with other programs, usually those produced by the same manufacturer, and can read the chart files of those programs, thus speeding up data entry.

The text to the many delineation packages on the market is built into the program and is usually written by a known astrologer or one with a flair for concise expression. In some cases, you may have a choice of authors or a choice of different texts, each slanted differently. Another option for the experienced astrologer is to write the text yourself. Using an editor program often supplied by the software company, you can get into the text database and re-compose delineations to suit your own style of thinking. With a little

---

15 I am the author of the text for Astrolabe's versatile Forecaster software which calculates and delineates transits, progressions and solar arc directions

effort you can personalize and customize an astrological report in a way that sets it apart from all others.

High-End Calculation Packages

These programs are for professionals who want the top-of-the-line software and most offer every conceivable kind of calculation known to astrologers. One of the real services these programs offer is the freedom to test out techniques. Over the centuries, numerous predictive and analytical techniques have been created and utilized, and in many cases no general consensus has ever been reached as to their validity or usefulness. With these programs, users can test for themselves if techniques like Ascendant arcs, or bodies like asteroids or fixed stars, work in a meaningful way for them. In this sense, astrological software has really opened all facets of astrology to testing by eliminating the incredibly time-consuming calculations necessary for most techniques. Most high-end calculation software also produces text reports, sometimes abbreviated versions, but some provide complete reports as add-ons. Programs in this category are usually in the upper price bracket, but you get a lot for your money.

Research Programs

One of the major problems that the field of astrology has faced over the past 300 years has been the lack of hard proof that it actually works. As described in Chapter 4, a major stumbling block for astrology was that proof by statistical analysis wasn't possible during the Scientific Revolution because those analytical techniques hadn't been invented yet. During the 20th century a few statistical studies of astrology were done, but at great expense in time and money to individuals. Because establishment scientists and academics continue to ignore astrology, no real money for research on the subject has been forthcoming. This is where a certain type of high-end calculation software comes in. For the first time in history, these programs allow individuals to do astrological research at a relatively low cost and with great potential benefit to the astrological and scientific communities.

Astrology software

Professional Interactive Programs

Today interactive programs are found online, as an app on a phone, and as a part of a larger software package. They meet the needs for users who require immediate responses to a wide number of options. With them the user is able quickly put a chart up on the screen, then manipulate it instantaneously to fit the needs of the moment. Such options are extremely valuable when doing horary astrology (answering questions as they are posed) or electional astrology (finding the best time to begin an action of one sort or another). More than anything else, interactive programs let the user experiment with astrology. Prices are usually somewhat lower than high-end calculation packages and some limited interactive apps can be downloaded from the internet for free. It is in this category that astrology software users can come closest to doing hands-on astrology. The immediate response to data entry allows for a kind of dialogue between user and machine.

Being able to access a quick answer to a question by reference to a chart for the moment (horary astrology), or to simply glance at where the planets are now, brings astrology closer to life. Having a chart for the present moment on screen (updating itself every ten seconds) can show amazing correlations with the world around us. Sometimes Mars will reach the MC and an interruption or loud noises will be heard; or when Uranus rises, a disruptive phone call comes through.

Specialized Astrology Programs

The field of astrology is really quite vast and there are a number of topics that require special software. One of the more popular branches of natal astrology today is astro-mapping. By casting a birth chart for a locality other than that of birth, a different set of houses is derived, and therefore a different planetary emphasis is created (see Chapter 8). Further, this information can be displayed graphically on a map, or on screen, and one can judge how visiting or moving to a particular location might be experienced. Today there are software packages that are strictly limited to the computations needed for the various methods of astro-mapping.

For hundreds of years astrologers have examined the positions of the planets placed on a circle called the astrological chart. Due to the graphics capability of modern computers, some programs offer alternatives to this perspective. Arranging planetary data in graph form lets one see more than just one moment in time – a graph makes the birth chart visibly dynamic. Such a revolution in astrology was really not possible without much effort and tedious hand calculations until the advent of the personal computer. Astrologers now have power tools that their predecessors never dreamed of.

Other specialty areas include programs that let users explore astrological traditions other than those of the Western world. Software from several producers is now available for Hindu (Vedic) astrology, a complex tradition that has never lost favor in India. The astrology of the Maya and Aztecs is the subject of Maya/Aztec Astro-Report, an Astrolabe program which is both screen-interactive and report-generating. As the author of the interpretation portion of this program, I can testify to its versatility and uniqueness among software packages.

Miscellaneous Software and Apps

Also available is a type of software which resides in your computer's memory or your mobile phone and can be called upon whenever you need it, regardless of what program you are running. By simply pressing a key, you can get a chart of the moment on a portion of your screen. With another keystroke, you get the aspects of the current planets. In some respects, this is like having access to a constantly moving astrological clock. Celeste from Astrolabe is an example.

A large number of apps based on astrology have proliferated in recent years and will, no doubt, continue to do so. Most of these are based around Sun-signs with some actually producing a natal chart. Others, including those listed below, do more including bringing you into networks of others where chart comparisons are provided for relationship evaluation. With these apps the marriage of artificial intelligence, astrology and heavy marketing yields questionable results for both individuals, relationships and the status of astrology.

costarastrology.com – This app calculates natal charts and offers interpretive information with an emphasis on relationships. It lists planets and signs, and it produces daily reports based on transits that consist of a line or two, but not the technical details. Users can learn things about technical astrology from the website.

thepattern.com – The Pattern is an app that provides information based on astrology, but doesn't use the terminology, which immediately solves one of the biggest problems astrology faces – its archaic vocabulary. What is generated by the app is then not so obviously linked to astrology making interpretations appear somewhat mysterious and magical. For an additional fee, more features become available to the user.

Astrologers may also want to investigate software that has been written for amateur astronomers. A number of low-cost programs are available today that calculate eclipses and lunations, and some even draw star maps. Much of this information is also available using some of the high-end astrological calculation packages, but some users may find these smaller astronomical programs interesting. Since they are designed for those interested in astronomy, their astrological uses may be limited, but the difference in approach may also be a stimulus to creative thinking about our cosmic environment. Free software like Stellarium, if you take the time to learn its many options, can teach you much about the correspondences between an astrological chart and the actual sky.

Astrological software is mostly purchased online today. Begin by looking at websites of the many companies and individuals that have products for sale or subscription. Once you've decided on what type of program you're interested in purchasing, you will most likely be able to download it for a free trial. Take your time to explore the potentials before committing to a payment. Make sure you feel comfortable with the product and the kind of support they offer.

The future of astrology and computers and other devices is promising. As these technologies become more powerful and easier to use, ideas that were once just dreams can become real and useful. In the future we may use expert systems whereby chart delineations read like that of an experienced astrologer. These programs will allow astrologers to transfer the exact way he or she reads a chart to the software. The marriage of astrology and computers promises to be not only fruitful but a powerful one as well.

Sources for Astrological Software

AIR Software. ww.alphee.com. AIR (Astrological Institode of Research) offers a wide variety of unique programs, many based on the work, research, and creative ideas of professional astrologer Alphee Lavoie.

Astrograph. https://www.astrograph.com. This is home of TimePassages astrology software, which for many years was one of the few written for the Apple operating system. A phone app is also available.

Astrolabe Software. www.alabe.com. A pioneer in software for astrologers that publishes the highly rated Solar Fire software. Astrolabe offers a complete line of tools for astrology and report writers and has a reputation for bug-free programs. The Celeste app draws a beautiful chart, runs on iPhone or android and is free.

AstroGold for Mac, iPhone and iPad app and android devices offers a more complete array of astrological calculations and delineations.

Cosmic Patterns. www.astrosoftware.com. A wide range of programs are available including the comprehensive Sirius and the versatile Kepler software packages. In addition a large number of report programs can be purchased to compliment calculation software.

Halloran Software. www.halloran.com. Quality programs at good prices.

Matrix Software. www.astrologysoftware.com. Software with a long history. Large programs like Win*Star and Blue*Star, and other more specialized report programs known for their versatility and excellent graphics are available.

Appendix C

Calculating an astrological chart

Doing serious astrology requires an accurate astrological chart, a map of the sky at a specific time and place. To calculate a chart three pieces of data are needed: the date, the time and the location. With this information and an ephemeris of planetary positions and table of houses, someone capable of doing arithmetic, comfortable working with degrees, minutes and seconds (sexagesimal notation), and using a calculator should be able to produce an accurate astrological chart in well under an hour. Until the advent of the computer, chart calculations had to be accomplished by hand. In the 1960s, I calculated charts using tables of proportions that I made myself. Later, I used either tables of logarithms or a slide rule. By the mid 1970s I was doing calculations on a scientific calculator using trig functions. At this point I could have a chart fully calculated in under 10 minutes. Not much later I got my first computer and left chart calculations behind – but I did not lose the deep understanding of the coordinate system astronomy that an astrological chart is based on. Even today many astrologers consider the knowledge that comes with doing chart calculations to be extremely useful, very helpful in matters of interpretation, and they are still required on some astrological certification exams.

A few basic concepts are essential in understanding what is actually done in calculating a chart. First, is knowing something about the celestial sphere, the way the sky around us is mapped. The sky overhead can be viewed as a dome that rises from the horizon and tops out directly above at what's called the zenith. The movements of the Sun, Moon and planets during the day and night are seen as moving along a track, the ecliptic, so named because

Calculating an astrological chart

only exactly on that track can an eclipse occur. The ecliptic is the center of the zodiac, a band extending about 8 degrees north and south of it. In the diagram below you will see the horizon and the directions. Imagine standing in the center of the diagram looking south with east on your left and west on your right. This is the view that is captured in an astrological chart (see Chapter 8) from the Northern hemisphere. Notice that the line drawn connecting the north and south points passes through the zenith – this line is the meridian. Also notice the celestial equator and ecliptic. The celestial equator is Earth's equator projected into space and it always connects exactly with the east and west points on the horizon. The ecliptic, which is tilted relative to the equator by 23.45 degrees (Earth's tilted axis) does not always rise exactly at the east and west points, except at the equinoxes. As Earth rotates, bodies on the ecliptic (Sun, Moon and planets) will rise in the east, culminate when they cross the meridian, set in the west and then cross the lower meridian. This is the daily or diurnal cycle that is mapped out by the astrological houses.

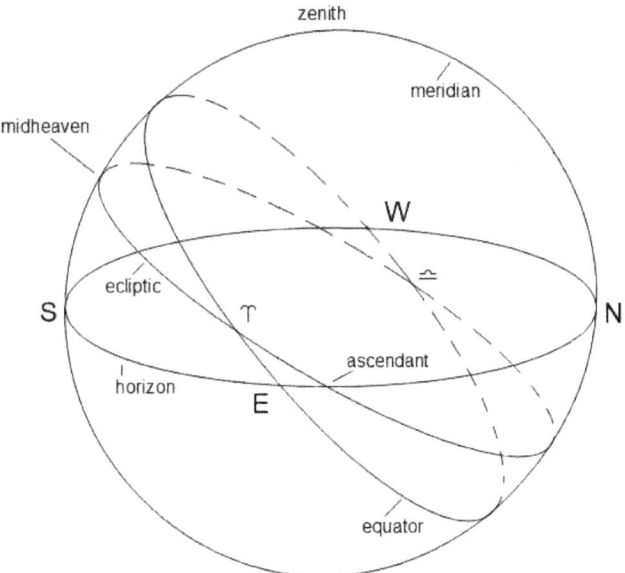

Figure 15. Celestial sphere

In order to calculate an astrological chart the motions of the celestial sphere must be captured at a single moment – the time of a birth or other event. When that has been accomplished, the positions of the planets in their diurnal cycle of rising and setting will be known. Because the ecliptic, the path of the planets, is divided into 12 sections the sign positions of each planet will also be known. Note that the zodiac begins at one of the two places where the equator and ecliptic intersect, indicated here by the Aries symbol. From this first degree of Aries, the zodiac extends 360 around the celestial sphere and is divided into 30 degree sections.

The following is a general description of what is involved in the calculation of an astrological chart. It is more of an outline and doesn't demonstrate step by step all that is necessary to produce a chart. Readers who wish to learn much more about this topic should consult my book *Astrological Chart Calculations*.

Tools for astrological chart calculations

At minimum you will need a midnight ephemeris (print or online) and a way to determine the geographical latitude and longitude of the place the chart will be calculated for. You will also need to know if daylight saving time was in effect as well. This information may be found online or from an astrological atlas that may also include latitudes and longitudes and other useful information. A table of houses (print or online) is another important tool in this work. In addition you will likely want to use a scientific calculator. It should have the trigonometric functions and an easy way of changing degrees and minutes into decimals, as well as the reverse. It should have at least one memory. Practice changing degrees (and minutes and seconds) to decimals and back again.

Calculating an astrological chart

What you will be doing:

A. Finding the GMT.

B. Finding the LST.

C. Finding the MC, Ascendant and house cusps from LST.

D. Calculating the planets' positions from GMT.

A: Finding the Greenwich Mean Time (GMT) of a birth or event.

1. Note the time of the event and correct it for daylight time (if it was in effect). This is usually minus 1 hour. Express the birth time in terms of 24 hours (military time).

2. Add the time zone difference for west longitude. Eastern Standard Time = +5 hours, CST = +6, etc. Subtract time zone difference for east longitudes.

3. This figure is the GMT. If it is greater than 24, subtract 24 and use the next day as the date of the birth or event.

Example: January 1, 2020 at 3:15 AM in NYC (time zone 5):
TIME (3:15) + Time Zone (5) = 8:15 = GMT

Summary: Birth Time +/- Time Zone = GMT

B. Finding the Local Sidereal Time (LST) of birth.

Sidereal time (ST) measures the rotation of Earth relative to the fixed stars that form the background to the moving bodies of the solar system. It is used to calculate the Ascendant and the houses. Sidereal time is standardized in Greenwich, England where 0 hour is set when 0 degrees of Aries crosses the meridian. Sidereal time is given in an ephemeris each day, most often at midnight. In the midnight ephemeris below you can see the sidereal time listed and that it changes daily by about four minutes.

GMT +00:00 Tropical Geocentric Long	S.T. hh:mm:ss	Moon ☽	Sun ☉	Mercury ☿	Venus ♀	Mars ♂	Jupiter ♃	Saturn ♄	Uranus ♅	Neptune ♆	Pluto ♇
Jan 1 2020	06:40:29	16°♓08'	10°♑00'	04°♑23'	14°♒24'	28°♏23'	06°♑40'	21°♑23'	02°♉41' ℞	16°♓15'	22°♑23'
Jan 2 2020	06:44:25	28°♓01'	11°♑01'	05°♑57'	15°♒38'	29°♏03'	06°♑54'	21°♑30'	02°♉41'	16°♓17'	22°♑25'
Jan 3 2020	06:48:22	09°♈53'	12°♑02'	07°♑32'	16°♒51'	29°♏43'	07°♑07'	21°♑37'	02°♉40'	16°♓18'	22°♑27'
Jan 4 2020	06:52:18	21°♈50'	13°♑04'	09°♑07'	18°♒04'	00°♐24'	07°♑21'	21°♑44'	02°♉40'	16°♓19'	22°♑29'
Jan 5 2020	06:56:15	03°♉55'	14°♑05'	10°♑43'	19°♒18'	01°♐04'	07°♑35'	21°♑51'	02°♉39'	16°♓20'	22°♑31'
Jan 6 2020	07:00:11	16°♉14'	15°♑06'	12°♑19'	20°♒31'	01°♐45'	07°♑49'	21°♑58'	02°♉39'	16°♓22'	22°♑33'
Jan 7 2020	07:04:08	28°♉50'	16°♑07'	13°♑55'	21°♒44'	02°♐25'	08°♑03'	22°♑06'	02°♉39'	16°♓23'	22°♑35'
Jan 8 2020	07:08:05	11°♊46'	17°♑08'	15°♑32'	22°♒58'	03°♐05'	08°♑16'	22°♑13'	02°♉39'	16°♓24'	22°♑37'
Jan 9 2020	07:12:01	25°♊04'	18°♑09'	17°♑09'	24°♒11'	03°♐46'	08°♑30'	22°♑20'	02°♉39'	16°♓26'	22°♑39'
Jan 10 2020	07:15:58	08°♋44'	19°♑10'	18°♑47'	25°♒24'	04°♐26'	08°♑44'	22°♑27'	02°♉39'	16°♓27'	22°♑41'
Jan 11 2020	07:19:54	22°♋44'	20°♑12'	20°♑25'	26°♒37'	05°♐07'	08°♑58'	22°♑34'	02°♉38'	16°♓28'	22°♑43'
Jan 12 2020	07:23:51	07°♌00'	21°♑13'	22°♑03'	27°♒50'	05°♐48'	09°♑11'	22°♑41'	02°♉39' D	16°♓30'	22°♑45'
Jan 13 2020	07:27:47	21°♌27'	22°♑14'	23°♑42'	29°♒03'	06°♐28'	09°♑25'	22°♑48'	02°♉39'	16°♓31'	22°♑47'
Jan 14 2020	07:31:44	06°♍00'	23°♑15'	25°♑22'	00°♓16'	07°♐09'	09°♑39'	22°♑55'	02°♉39'	16°♓33'	22°♑49'
Jan 15 2020	07:35:40	20°♍31'	24°♑16'	27°♑02'	01°♓29'	07°♐49'	09°♑52'	23°♑02'	02°♉39'	16°♓34'	22°♑51'

1. From the ephemeris, find the Sidereal Time (ST) at midnight on the day of birth. In the sample above, the ST for January 1 (06:40:29) is listed after the date and before the Moon, Sun and planet positions.

2. Add the GMT to the ST.

3. Add the solar-sidereal correction (SCC). Because the Sun moves ahead in the zodiac about a degree per day, and because our clocks and calendar require the Sun to be overhead every day around noon, an adjustment must be made to the sidereal time that is called the solar-sidereal correction (SSC). This figure is roughly equivalent to 10 seconds per hour or 240 seconds per day, a figure that is always less than 4 minutes of time per day. The GMT above of 8:15 would amount to 80 seconds for the 8 hours and 2 or 3 seconds for the additional 15 minutes. The resultant figure, let's say 82 seconds or 1 minute and 12 seconds, is then added to the sum of the ST and GMT.

4. Sidereal time from an ephemeris is the sidereal time at Greenwich, England, so if you are anywhere else you will need to make an adjustment to the geographical longitude. This is done by first converting the degrees and minutes of longitude into time: 15 degrees of geographical longitude = 1 hour clock time. The

conversion of longitude to time is called the longitude-time equivalent or LTE. For example, the longitude of NYC is 74.006 degrees west. At 1 hour per 15 degrees of longitude this would be just under 5 hours – 74.006 divided by 15 = 4 hours and 56 minutes and 1 second (expressed as 4:56:01 or 4h 56m 01s). For the longitude of Washington, D.C., 77.0369, divide the figure by 15 to get 5.1358 and then convert to degrees, minutes and seconds on the calculator. The result is 5:08:09 or 5h 8m 9s.

From the sum of ST, GMT and SSC, subtract the LTE if the location was west of Greenwich or add if east of Greenwich. The formula for the LST is then ST + GMT + SSC +/- LTE.

When the equation is worked the resultant figure is the local sidereal time or LST. The Ascendant and houses of an astrological chart are calculated from the LST, the planet positions are calculated from the GMT.

Summary: Birth Time +/- Zone = GMT
ST + GMT + SSC +/- LTE = LST

Example: January 1, 2020 at 3:15 AM in NYC. GMT = 8:15

ST (06:40:29) + GMT (8:15:00) + SSC (00:01:12) – LTE (4:56:01) = 10:00:40

The calculated LST is then used to determine the Ascendant and the house cusps. The easiest way to find these is by using a table of houses (print or online) for the geographical latitude of the event. Here is a piece of a table of houses.

Sid.Time: 10h00m = MC: 27 ♌ 49'07

Lat	11	12	Asc	2	3
40N	0 ♎ 00	26 ♎ 10	17 ♏ 32	17 ♐ 18	21 ♑ 45
41N	0 ♎ 00	25 ♎ 59	17 ♏ 06	16 ♐ 51	21 ♑ 30

Since the calculated LST is almost exactly 10 hours, this portion of the table shows that the MC will be at 27 degrees and 49 minutes of Leo. But the LST is actually 10 hours 0 minutes and 41 seconds and the seconds would need to be accounted for by going to the next listing (which is 10:04) and then working out the difference. Similar adjustments will need to be made for the Ascendant, which is the cusp of the first house. Here the Ascendant at 40 north latitude and 42 north latitude are given, but the latitude of NYC is 40 degrees and 43 minutes, so the proportional difference must be calculated using arithmetic. The same adjustments need to be done for the houses as well. The cusp of the 10th is the MC and the cusp of the 4th is exactly opposite the MC. Likewise, the cusps for houses 11, 12, 2 and 3, which are given, are exactly opposite the cusps of houses 5, 6, 8 and 9 – so no calculation is needed for them, just a proper sign adjustment.

Solving for a precise MC, Ascendant and house cusps can be done with proportions, logarithms or, most commonly, with tables made especially for this work. In regard to house cusps, many astrologers use what are called equal houses which radiate from the Ascendant at 30 degree intervals. Another method, commonly used in ancient times, are whole sign houses which simply use the first degree of the sign of the Ascendant as the cusp of the first house. A third traditional method is to trisect the arc between the MC and Ascendant, and Ascendant and IC, this being the Porphyry method. All other methods are complicated and require special tables or lengthy trigonometrical calculations. There is no consensus in the astrological community as to the utility of these methods for interpretation.

D. Calculating the Planets' Places

To calculate the exact positions of the planets you will need an ephemeris and the figure for the GMT. Basically, you will be solving for a proportion, that is taking how far each planet traveled in one day (its daily motion) and then finding how far it traveled up to the moment of birth, which is what

Calculating an astrological chart

the GMT is. For the Sun, Moon, and inner planets, use the rules below. You should be able to estimate the positions of the outer planets in your head.

1. Divide the GMT (in decimals) by 24. Store this figure, called the Constant Fraction (CF), in your calculator's memory. In the example, the GMT is 8:15 or expressed as a decimal, 8.25. Dividing this figure by 24 = 0.3437, which is the fraction into the day of the GMT.

2. Calculate the daily motion of the planet in question according to the following formula: Daily Motion = the planet's longitude in the ephemeris on the day after the birth (later longitude) minus its longitude on the day of birth (earlier longitude). For the example of January 1, we see the Sun, in Capricorn, is listed as 11° 01' on January 2. We then subtract from it the Sun's position on January 1 (10° 00') and get a difference of 1 degree and 1 minute, or 61 minutes.

3. Multiply the daily motion of the planet by the constant fraction in your calculator's memory. (61 x 0.3437 = 21 minutes)

4. Take the result of step #3 and add it to the planet's longitude on the day of birth (earlier longitude). This equals the planets zodiacal position exactly. For the example: 10° 00' + 00° 21' = 10° 21' or 10 degrees and 21 minutes of Capricorn.

You may come across a few quirks now and then and will need to solve the problem a bit differently – there may be several ways to get the correct result. One is in regard to the two longitude positions being in different signs. Another quirk is in regard to retrogradation. These will require adjustments in adding and subtracting, but with some thought can be handled easily. The calculations for the Moon and planets follows the same logic. Once these have been calculated, they are placed into the framework of the chart set by the houses.

In doing calculations it is useful to use the true longitude of the zodiac signs, that is the total distance from the beginning of the zodiac at 0 degrees Aries. Below is a list of signs, and the degrees they begin with, which you should become familiar with. To convert a figure in true longitude to zodiacal sign and degree, simply subtract the closest lesser value below. Example: 118 degrees. Cancer at 90 degrees is the closest lesser value, so 118 minus 90 equals 28, or 28 degrees of Cancer.

Aries: 0	Leo: 120	Sagittarius: 240
Taurus: 30	Virgo: 150	Capricorn: 270
Gemini: 60	Libra: 180	Aquarius: 300
Cancer: 90	Scorpio: 210	Pisces: 330

In summary, astrological chart calculation is not particularly difficult, but it does involve a series of solutions that need to be done more or less in order. The most difficult, and time-consuming, calculations are those for the MC and Ascendant, and the house cusps. These problems of proportions are usually handled with interpolation tables. One alternative is to use trigonometric formulae. With a low-cost entry-level scientific calculator and some care when inputting data, this method is by far the fastest. You will need to use these variables, however.

RAMC (Right Ascension of the MC) is the Local Sidereal Time expressed as degrees and minutes.
RAMC = LST x 15

OBL (obliquity) is a constant as it is the tilt of Earth's axis.
OBL = 23.45

LAT = geographic latitude, expressed as a decimal.
Example: 40 N 43 or 40.72

The formula for calculating the MC is:

$$\text{ARC tan } \frac{\tan \text{RAMC}}{\cos \text{OBL}}$$

The formula for calculating the Ascendant is:

$$\frac{(\tan \text{LAT.} \times \sin \text{OBL}) + (\sin \text{RAMC} \times \cos \text{OBL})}{\cos \text{RAMC}} \times (-1) \; 1/X \text{ ARC tan}$$

The Ascendant calculation will produce an exact figure but the actual quadrant of the zodiac may in some cases need to be adjusted by adding either 180 or 360. By having an idea of where the Ascendant should be (based on where the MC is) you will know whether to adjust and how much to add.

Chart Calculation Resources

The American Ephemeris (ACS Publications). Very complete, accurate and easy to read. *The American Ephemeris for the 20th Century* (Midnight) has the entire century in one paperbound volume. *The American Ephemeris for the 21st Century* covers 2001 to 2050.

The American Ephemeris 1950-2050 at Midnight by Neil F. Michelsen.

The New American Ephemeris for the 21st Century, 2000-2100 at Midnight by Rique Pottenger.

The New American Ephemeris 2020-2030: *Longitude, Declination & Latitude* by Rique Pottenger.

The Astrolabe World Ephemeris: 2001-2050 At Midnight Schiffer Publishing (January 1, 2000) by Robert Hand.

World Ephemeris: 20th Century, Midnight Schiffer; 1st edition 1997.

Raphael's Astronomical Ephemeris of the Planets' Places for 2020 (and other single years): A Complete Aspectarian and tables of houses for London and NY. Foulsham & Co Ltd.

Scofield, Bruce. *Astrological Chart Calculations.* The Wessex Astrologer 2021.

House Tables:

The American Book of Tables (ACS Publications). Includes Placidus and Koch house tables, other useful tables, and detailed instructions on how to cast a chart. Another version of this is *The Michelsen Book of Tables.* August 1, 1997. by Neil F. Michelsen (Compiler), Rique Pottenger.

Appendix D

An Astrological Resource Directory

Websites

Astrology has permeated the internet, but most of it is commerce-driven and limited to Sun-signs. Almost all of these are identified as "horoscopes", a term they use incorrectly. Probably thousands of people with cosmic names compete with each other in the cyber marketplace to sell basically the same products – reports on love, money and success. There are a number of websites hosted by some very competent astrologers, however. Some offer much in the way of real knowledge in the form of articles, podcasts, and videos, some hold classes and may offer personal readings. Here are two multi-faceted ones.

www.astro.com – This website is called Astrodienst, which means "astro service" in German, though it is a Swiss company founded by Alois Treindl who holds a PhD in physics. It has been operating for several decades and, in my opinion, has put together a platform that serves a very wide range of astrological needs. The novice will find Sun-sign reports, intermediate astrologers will find many articles and professionals will use the data in the very large astro-databank of charts. The website allows one to calculate a chart accurately and use an online ephemeris and table of houses if you want to do your own calculations.

www.astrotheme.com – Like astro.com, this website offers a range of popular "horoscope" information, but it includes a very large collection of celebrity natal charts. Philippe Lepoivre de Vesle, an French engineer and scientific researcher, is the founder of the website and he has devised a number of interesting statistical applications to popular astrology, particularly in the analysis of the many charts in the database.

Books

Books have long been the primary method of learning astrology. There are many books on astrology available today in both print and ebook form covering every aspect of the subject. With the subject of astrology, newer doesn't necessarily mean better, so be sure to take a look at some older titles too. Many astrology books can be read online from websites like Internet Archive and Open Library. Among the leading publishers of astrology books are ACS, Llewellyn, Para Research, AFA, Foulsham, Inner Traditions, The Wessex Astrologer etc. Below are just a recommended few.

Astrology and science
Boxer, Alexander. *A Scheme of Heaven: The History of Astrology and the Search for our Destiny in Data*. Norton, 2020. The author, a data scientist, offers a good description of astrology and its history from the perspective of an outsider. He doesn't think the subject actually works, however, and explains it away in terms of statistics and randomness. Interestingly, he offers his birth data which describes, in no uncertain terms, that of a skeptic.

Michel Gauquelin. *Birth-Times*. Hill and Wang, 1983. This is only one of many books by Gauquelin that describe his methods of testing astrology. Other titles include *The Cosmic Clocks, The Scientific Basis of Astrology,* and *Planetary Heredity*.

The history of astrology
Benson Bobrick *The Fated Sky: Astrology in History*. Simon & Schuster, 2006. This is a good, all around, and very entertaining account of astrology from ancient times to the present.

Nicholas Campion. *A History of Western Astrology: Volumes I and II.* Continuum, 2009. Here is a massive, thorough and very deep account of astrology from pre-historic times to the present that is focused primarily on its social and cultural history.

S.J. Tester. *A History of Western Astrology.* Ballantine Books, 1987. This is a serious, academic study of astrology from ancient times to the Renaissance.

The fundamentals of astrology

C.E.O. Carter. *Principles of Astrology.* Theosophical Publishing House, Ltd., 1971. A classic primer of astrology from one of England's finest early 20th century astrologers.

Ronald Davison. *Astrology: The Classic Guide to Understanding Your Horoscope.* Bell, 1963. This book has seen many printings and continues to be a classic on the elements of astrology.

Sue Farebrother. *Astrology Decoded: A Step by Step Guide to Learning Astrology.* Rider, 2013. A practical and comprehensive course that will take you through from the 12 zodiac signs to subtle astrological combinations and aspects. Ideal for a beginner.

Robert Hand. *Horoscope Symbols.* Whitford Press, 1981. Every symbol used by practicing astrologers is explained clearly and pragmatically without neglecting the psychological and spiritual dimensions.

Deborah Houlding. *The Houses: Temples of the Sky.* The Wessex Astrologer, 2006. An excellent, if very slim book, from this renowned traditional astrologer that gives the background to the house systems along with interpretations. Required reading for many courses.

Lee Lehman. *Classical Astrology for Modern Living: From Ptolemy to Psychology & Back Again.* Schiffer, 2000. Here is a good account of what traditional astrology was, and is, and what to do with it. The author has written many other interesting books for intermediate and professional astrologers.

Jeff Mayo. *A Key to Personality*. C. W. Daniel 2009. Here is a book for beginners wanting simple instructions on how to interpret a chart, as well as for old hands seeking fresh perspectives, an unusually clear and rational view of astrology's multilevel perspective on the human condition.

Marion D. March and Joan McEvers, *The Only Way to Learn Astrology*. ACS 2009. An excellent series of six books, with each one having a different theme – horary, forecasting etc.

Kim Rodgers-Gallagher. *Astrology for the Light Side of the Brain*. ACS, 1994. This hilarious book covers nearly all sides of astrology. Out of print but available in some areas.

Dane Rudhyar. *The Astrological Houses*, Doubleday, 1972, and *Astrological Signs*, Shambala, 1963. A more recent printing titled *The Twelve Astrological Houses* is available. Rudhyar's many writings on astrology have a philosophical slant and have influenced several generations of astrologers.

Dictionaries of astrology
Nicholas DeVore. *Encyclopedia of Astrology*. Philosophical Library, 1947, 2005. This is a comprehensive and sometimes technical collection of astrological descriptions that has aged very well.

Derek and Julia Parker. *Parkers Encyclopedia of Astrology*. Watkins 2009. An excellent walk-through of astrology's fascinating history, packed with anecdotes and facts that will make you want to learn more. See also *Parkers Astrology* for a good beginner introduction.

Donna Woodwell. *The Astrology Dictionary: Cosmic Knowledge from A to Z*. Adams Media, 2019. A small book, but good for beginners.

Psychological astrology

Stephen Arroyo. *Astrology, Karma & Transformation: The Inner Dimensions of the Birth Chart*. CRCS, 2013. This is a new edition of a classic work on psychological astrology.

Steven Forrest. *The Inner Sky*. ACS, 1985. In this and other books, among them *The Changing Sky* and *The Night Speaks*, Forrest writes passionately and philosophically on how astrology encourages free-will and choice.

Liz Greene and Howard Sasportas. *The Development of the Personality*. Samuel Weiser, 1987, and *The Dynamics of the Unconscious*. Samuel Weiser, 1988. These two books are transcriptions of seminars on psychological astrology presented by two masters. See also other works by Liz Greene.

Clare Martin. *Mapping the Psyche: An Introduction to Psychological Astrology*. Transcribed from lectures held at the Centre for Psychological Astrology and presented in a seminar format, volumes 1, 2 and 3 give a firm grounding in all aspects of psychological astrology. The Wessex Astrologer.

Dane Rudhyar. *The Astrology of Personality*. Doubleday, 1936, 1970. This is the first of many books Rudhyar wrote on astrology. In it he approaches astrology from a philosophical, psychological, and spiritual perspective.

Richard Tarnas. *Cosmos and Psyche: Intimations of a New World View*. Plume, 2006. In this large work, Jungian concepts in astrology are explored in terms of history and cultural evolution.

Relationships

Brian Clark. *From the Moment We Met: The Astrology of Adult Relationships*. LSA/Flare, 2018. A mythological and archetypal perspective toward relationships is applied to natal charts and synastry.

Ronald Davison. *Synastry*. Aurora Press, 1983. A guidebook to traditional chart comparisons, planet by planet.

Robert Hand. *Planets in Composite*. Para Research, 1975. A guide to the meanings of the planets in a chart derived from two birth charts.

Richard Idemon. *Through the Looking Glass*. The Wessex Astrologer, 2010. This astro-psychology book approaches relationships as reflections of our inner selves.

Transits and forecasting

Sue Farebrother. *Astrology Forecasting: The Expert Guide to Astrological Prediction*. Rider 2019. An in-depth guide to the calculations behind forecasting. Not a cookbook, excellent for serious astrology students.

Martin Gansten. *Primary Directions: Astrology's Old Master Techniques* (2019), see also *Annual Predictive Techniques of the Greek, Arabic and Indian Astrologers* (2020). The Wessex Astrologer. In-depth calculations for forecasting - ideal for serious astrologers looking to hone their predictive techniques.

Hand, Robert. *Planets in Transit*. Whitford Press, 1976. An excellent astrological "cookbook" for interpreting transits.

April Elliott Kent. *Astrological Transits: The Beginner's Guide to Using Planetary Cycles to Plan and Predict Your Day, Week, Year (or Destiny)*. Crestline Books, 2020. An introduction to transits and their interpretations.

Anthony Louis. *The Art of Forecasting Using Solar Returns*. The Wessex Astrologer 2008. The nuts and bolts of solar returns, with plentiful case studies as examples.

Celeste Teal. *Predicting Events With Astrology*. Llewellyn, 2009. An introduction to a few of astrology's predictive techniques.

An Astrological Resource Directory

Useful and Informative websites and print periodicals

http://astrologynewsservice.com. This is a joint project of the astrological associations ISAR, NCGR, AFA and AFAN and publishes short articles about astrology as it relates to the larger culture.

Llewellyn's Astrological Calendar, Moon Sign Book, Sun Sign Book and Daily Planetary Guide. All of these are published annually by Llewellyn Publications. All offer useful astrological information about the year ahead, articles by leading astrologers, and much more.

The Astrological Journal. The bi-monthly magazine of the Astrological Association, featuring articles from astrologers around the world. Details on their website - see below.

The Mountain Astrologer www.mountainastrologer.com – America's best astrology magazine, with great articles on current topics, theme issues, humor, reviews.

Astrological Organizations and Schools

Most of these have online bookshops, and offer online courses and webinars internationally as well as regular conferences. Check individual websites for details:

American Federation of Astrologers (AFA) www.astrologers.com

Association for Astrological Networking (AFAN) www.afan.org

Astrological Association of Great Britain (AA) www.astrologicalassociation.com

Astrology University www.astrologyuniversity.com

Faculty of Astrological Studies www.astrology.org.uk

What Astrology is ...And How to Use it

Federation of Australian Astrologers (FAA) www.faainc.org.au

International Academy of Astrology (IAA) www.astrocollege.org

International Society for Astrological Research (ISAR) www.isarastrology.com

Kepler College www.keplercollege.org

London School of Astrology (LSA) www.londonschoolofastrology.co.uk

Mayo School of Astrology www.mayoastrology.com

Mercury Internet School of Psychological Astrology (MISPA) www.mercuryinternetschool.com

National Center for Geocosmic Research (NCGR) www.geocosmic.org

Organisation for Professional Astrology (OPA) www.opaastrology.org

QHP School of Astrology www.qhpastrology.co.uk

School of Traditional Astrology www.sta.co

Blank forms

	Asc	Su	Mo	Me	Ve	Ma	Ju	Sa	Ur	Ne	Pl
Base score	3	3	3	2	2	2	1	1	1	1	1
Angular											
Elevated											
Asc ruler											
P-Score											

Sign	Asc	Su	Mo	Me	Ve	Ma	Ju	Sa	Ur	Ne	Pl	Z-Score
Aries												
Taurus												
Gemini												
Cancer												
Leo												
Virgo												
Libra												
Scorpio												
Sagittarius												
Capricorn												
Aquarius												
Pisces												

Fire	
Earth	
Air	
Water	

Cardinal	
Fixed	
Mutable	

Above	
Below	

East	
West	

		a.	b.	c.	total		a.	b.	c.	total
1	Self-directed					Other-directed				
2	Thinker					Feeler				
3	Flexible					Rigid				
4	Practical					Idealistic				
5	Extraverted					Introverted				
6	Controlled					Reactive				
7	Leader					Cooperater				
8	Organized					Chaotic				
9	Extremist					Moderate				
10	Conservative					Progressive				

www.ingramcontent.com/pod-product-compliance
Lightning Source LLC
Chambersburg PA
CBHW061939220426
43662CB00012B/1964